Beginners Backyard Beekeeping Made Easy

By Beekeeping Guidebooks

Foreword

Foreword

The wonderful world of beekeeping is suitable for everybody, whether you live in a busy city, the suburbs or in the countryside.

Enjoy the buzzing sound of bees in your backyard and on hot days, you will have the majestic smell of honey wafting through the air.

Your bees will increase pollination in your yard. This means that yields from fruit trees and all fruits and vegetables will increase. You may also harvest honey beeswax, pollen, and propolis from the hive.

The honey will be delicious, and you will have so much that you can share it with family, friends and neighbors and still have plenty for yourself.

Some beekeepers even make a profit from the honey produced.

The brilliant thing is that it is not too complicated. The bees know what they are doing – you simply need to provide them with a good place to live and help them out from time to time.

You are already interested in bees so now is the time to explore the world of apiculture.

Foreword

Table of Contents

Table of Contents

Foreword 2

Table of Contents 4

Chapter One - Introduction to Beekeeping 10

    Why are Bees So Important?.. 11

    Decline of the Bees 13

    Causes of the Honey Bee Decline 14

    Insecticides 15

    Colony Collapse Disorder.. 15

Chapter 2 – All About the Honey Bee................................ 17

    Physical Appearance 18

    Anatomy of the Bee... 18

    How do Bees Fly?.. 19

    What do Honey Bees See?... 20

    The Sting of a Bee 20

    Bee 'Beehavior' 21

    The Honey Bee Colony.. 22

    Type of Bees 23

    Swarms 24

Chapter 3 – How Can We Help Our Bees?......................... 26

    Become a Beekeeper.. 26

    Help to Protect Swarms... 27

Table of Contents

    Plant Bee Friendly Plants 28

    Purchase Local Honey 30

    Bee Friendly 30

Chapter 4 – What All Beekeepers Must Know 31

    Beekeeping and the Law 31

    How Much Time Does Beekeeping Take Up? 32

    Scientific Names for Honey Bees 34

    Why Do Bees Sting? 35

    How Honey Bees Communicate 36

    Honey Bee Pheromones 36

    Dance of the Honey Bee 37

    What Do Honey Bees Eat? 39

    Lifespan of the Honey Bee 40

Chapter 5 – Exploring the Different Species 42

    Western Honey Bee 42

    European Dark Bee 43

    Italian Bee 45

    Carniolan Bee 47

    Caucasian Bee 49

    Buckfast Bee 50

    The Russian Bee 52

    The Giant Honey Bee 54

Table of Contents

    Africanized Honey Bee.. 55

Chapter 6 – All About Honey... 57

    How Do Bees Make Honey?... 57

    Why Do Bees Make Honey? 60

    Beeswax 62

    How Much Honey?.. 64

    Different Types of Honey 64

Chapter 7 – A History of Beekeeping... 66

    Gum Hives 66

    Early Beehive Designs 67

    Movable Comb Hives 68

    The Work of L.L. Langstroth 70

    Mass Production by A.I. Root 71

    Modern Beekeeping... 72

Chapter 8 - Placing Your Hives.. 74

    Locating the Perfect Place 74

    Seek 'Light Shade' 75

    Dry, Level Ground 76

    Water and Vegetation 76

    Convenient Access 77

    Urban Beekeeping.. 79

Chapter 9 – Beekeepers at Work... 81

Table of Contents

- The Beekeeping Community 81
- Your First Beehives 83
- Buying Hive Kits 84
- To Paint or Not to Paint? 86
- Creating Your Bee Yard 87
- Working from the Bottom Up 88
- Hive Tools 90
- Entrance Reducer 91

Chapter 10 – Introducing the Bees to Your Hive 93
- Buying a Package of Bees 93
- The Arrival of Your Bees 94
- Handling the Queen Cage 95
- Releasing the Bees 96
- Installing a Hive Top Feeder 97
- Hydration for Your Bees 98
- Checking the Queen Release 98
- Protective Clothing 99

Chapter 11 - Inspecting Your Hives 100
- The Bee Smoker 100
- Performing an Inspection 101
- Adding the Upper Deep" 103
- Removing the Entrance Reducer 103

Table of Contents

    The Queen Excluder and Honey Supers 104

    Ventilation and Cooling 105

    Dealing with Bee Stings 106

Chapter 12 – Harvesting Your Honey 107

    A Word of Sticky Warning 107

    The Debate Over Honeycomb 108

    Removing the Frames from the Hive 110

    Uncapping the Frames 111

    The Honey Extractor 112

    Grading and Storing Honey 114

Chapter 13 – The Changing Seasons 116

    Survival of the Colony 116

    Early Spring 117

    Essential Winter Ventilation 117

    Preparing for Winter 118

    Checking Your Bees in Winter 120

Chapter 14 – Recipes for your Bees 121

    The Problem with Honey 122

    Bees Love Sugar Syrup 122

    Supplement Spring Feeding 123

    Supplement Winter Feeding 124

    Stimulate Brood Rearing 126

Table of Contents

    Dry Pollen Substitute 126

    Pollen Patty 127

    Grease Patties 127

Chapter 15 – Honey Bee Health 130

    Varroa Mites 131

    Tracheal Acarine Mites 132

    Nosema 132

    Small Hive Beetle 133

    Wax Moths 133

    Foulbrood 134

    Chalkbrood 135

    Stonebrood 135

    Other Health Threats 136

    The Risk of Colony Collapse Disorder 136

Afterword 138

Relevant Websites 141

Glossary 144

Index 157

Chapter One - Introduction to Beekeeping

Chapter One - Introduction to Beekeeping

There are many reasons people become interested in beekeeping. Contrary to the often-fearful perception of humans, bees are, by nature, gentle and hardworking. Watching and interacting with them is truly mesmerizing.

You will discover that beekeeping is a most enjoyable, stimulating and captivating hobby. Plus, you get to eat your own honey too – highly satisfying and rewarding.

Honeybees are under threat on a global scale and need our help to survive. This makes beekeeping tremendously important.

In the wild, virtually all the colonies had already died out. Without beekeepers to care for them, we could see the disappearance of honey bees in just a few years.

Chapter One - Introduction to Beekeeping

Beekeeping is a wonderful way to help boost the bee population and is one of the few hobbies that will have such a beneficial impact – you can play an important part in saving these unique creatures.

Why are Bees So Important?

On our planet, there are more than 20,000 species of bees. Indigenous to different areas all over the world, all the different types of bees make their own unique contribution to our ecosystem.

Crops, from fruit and vegetables, to coffee and tea, all rely on bees. There are more honey bees than other types of bee and pollinating insects. This makes the honey bee the world's most significant pollinator of food crops. There are many species of butterflies, flies, moths, wasps, beetles, birds, bats and other animals that also contribute to pollination.

Albert Einstein said, "if the bee disappeared off the surface of the globe then man would only have four years left to live". This may well be true.

At least one third of our food depends on pollination by the honey bee. Without doubt, humankind relies on the existence of bees. And their economic contribution is so vast that even from an economic viewpoint, it is worth protecting our bees.

- 75% of the world's food crops depend, to some extent, on pollination.

Chapter One - Introduction to Beekeeping

- Economic value of bees' pollination work has been estimated at around €265 billion annually, worldwide.

- The tiny alfalfa leafcutter bee alone is responsible for $7 billion of that amount created by pollinating the hay and alfalfa crops on which the cattle industry relies.

- Almost 90% of wild flowering plants depends, at least in part, on bee pollination.

- 1.6 million tons of honey produced annually from the Western honey bee.

- 40% of invertebrate pollinator species, especially bees and butterflies face extinction.

Chapter One - Introduction to Beekeeping

The survival of bees is intimately tied to the survival of humans – life without pollinators would be incredibly devastating for food production.

Crops that rely on bee pollination include those that provide fruit, vegetables, seeds, nuts and oils. Many of these are an essential source of vitamins and minerals. Without these crops, the likelihood of malnutrition will increase dramatically. Additionally, many developing countries rely on the income from coffee and cocoa production, which is reliant on bee pollination.

As well as food crops, other essential crops are also dependent on bee pollination. This includes crops that provide biofuels (e.g. canola and palm oil), fibers (e.g. cotton), medicines, foodstuffs for livestock and even construction materials.

Decline of the Bees

In recent years, honey bees have been dying off in large and unexplained numbers.

In North America, the National Agriculture Statistics Service reported that there were 2.44 million honey producing hives in the United States in February 2008. This was down from 4.5 million in 1980 and 5.9 million in 1947.

The U.S. Department of Agriculture reports that from 2006-2011 about 33% of bees perished annually. Since the 1990's, beekeepers around the world have been reporting a sudden and unexplained disappearance of bees and significant

Chapter One - Introduction to Beekeeping

reduction in honey bee colonies.

In 2010, The US Department of Agriculture reported that there had been an estimated 34% drop in the numbers of honey bees. This was statistically similar in 2007, 2008 and 2009. In 2011, the loss was estimated at 30%. In 2012-2013, Colony Collapse Disorder occurred in about half the loss of the honey bee hives.

The problem is on a global scale. The Canadian province of Manitoba lost 46% of it honey bee colonies in the winter of 2013 – this is a major agricultural area. Nationally, in the same year, Canada reported that approximately 29% of their bee colonies were lost. In 2008, The British Beekeepers Association reported that the bee population in the United Kingdom had dropped by around 30% between 2007 and 2008.

Causes of the Honey Bee Decline

The main reasons for global bee decline are related to industrial agriculture, parasites / pathogens and climate change. Bee killing pesticides have the most direct impact on honeybee decline.

The loss of biodiversity due to monocultures and the common use of bee killing pesticides pose real threats for honeybees and other wild pollinators.

Chapter One - Introduction to Beekeeping

Insecticides

These are chemicals which are designed to kill insects. They are widely used, particularly around cropland areas.

In our current chemical intensive agricultural methods, some insecticides are exhibiting clear, negative implications on the health of pollinators. This is having a devastating impact on both individual bees and bee colonies.

Colony Collapse Disorder

Colony Collapse Disorder occurs when most worker bees in a colony disappear – leaving behind only a queen, plenty of food and a small number of bees to care for the remaining larvae and pupa (and the queen).

These disappearances have been known to happen throughout the history of beekeeping. In the past this has been referred to as disappearing disease, spring dwindle, May disease, autumn collapse and fall dwindle disease.

The term Colony Collapse Disorder became established in 2006 and marked a dramatic rise in the decline of honey bee colonies in North America and throughout Europe. The new term recognized the fact that the phenomenon was not restricted to certain seasons.

Chapter One - Introduction to Beekeeping

Between 2007 and 2013, more than 10 million beehives were lost, often to Colony Collapse Disorder. This was almost twice the normal rate of loss.

It is thought that numerous factors have led to an increase in Colony Collapse Disorder – including pesticides, diseases, mites, malnutrition, genetic factors, immunodeficiencies, loss of habitat, changing beekeeping practices. It seems likely that it has been affected by a combination of these circumstances.

Chapter 2 – All About the Honey Bee

Chapter 2 – All About the Honey Bee

To be the best beekeeper you can be, it is both fascinating and of crucial importance to understand the physical makeup of the bee and the way that they live and socialize.

The honey bee (Apis Mellifera) is a social insect. They live in colonies where all the individual bees belong to the same family. Very often all offspring derive from the same mother. In the larger colonies, society is highly organized

Chapter 2 – All About the Honey Bee

where individual bees all have a specific role in the working of the colony.

Physical Appearance

Honey bees are about 15 mm long and are oval shaped. They have golden – yellow and brown bands of color. The body color of the honey bee varies between species – some honey bees have predominately black bodies – but virtually all have varying dark to light stripes.

The bright color and the dark and light stripes serve as protection for the honey bee against predators. Their bright colors warn of their ability to sting.

Anatomy of the Bee

The body of the bee is made up segments; stinger, legs, antenna, three sections of thorax and six visible sections of abdomen.

The head of the honey bee contains the eyes, antenna and feeding mechanisms. The purpose of the antenna is to smell / locate odors and to measure speed of flight. The bee's jaw is known as the mandible. This is used in eating pollen, cutting and shaping wax, feeding larvae and the queen, cleaning the hive, grooming and fighting.

Chapter 2 – All About the Honey Bee

The thorax of the honey bee is comprised of the wings, legs and the muscles. Together, these control movement. The forewing (usually larger than the hind wing) is used for flight and to keep cool. The hindwing is used to fan away heat and keep the beehive cool.

The six segments of the abdomen contain the female reproductive organs in the queen, male reproductive organs in the drone and the stinger in both workers and queens.

How do Bees Fly?

According to its size and the comparative size of its wings, the honey bee should not in theory, be capable of flying. It is one of nature's fascinating anomalies.

However, the honey bee skillfully and very efficiently flies from flower to flower, collecting pollen. In this way, the bee pollinates plants and trees as is it travels. So not only can it fly fast, it is able to perform a variety of functions as it does so.

Chapter 2 – All About the Honey Bee

What do Honey Bees See?

The honey bee has compound eyes. These are made up of many smaller eyes which all receive different images. The arthropod (e.g., insects, crustaceans) eye is built very differently to our own (and other vertebrate eyes). The smaller eyes are effectively repeating units (the ommatidia), each of which operates as an individual visual receptor.

The bee's brain comprises these images to make one complete picture.

Interestingly, vision varies between types of bees. Indeed, the drone bee (males) have larger eyes than the other bees. This is so that they can spot queen bees on their mating flight – this is the flight taken by a virgin queen during which she mates with several drones, all while remaining airborne.

The Sting of a Bee

When a honey bee stings a person, it is actually injecting venom (a poisonous substance) into its victim.

The stinger of the honey bee is attached to its abdomen. If a bee stings a person, the stinger can catch and consequently rip out the abdomen of the bee – this will result in death. However, it seems that if the bee happens to sting someone with thin skin, it can sometimes be that the stinger doesn't catch and therefore the bee will not die.

Chapter 2 – All About the Honey Bee

It is only the female honey bee that has the capacity to sting as the males do not have a stinger.

Bee 'Beehavior'

In the natural environment, honey bee hives are frequently situated in the holes of trees and on rock crevices.

The hive is comprised of wax which comes from the special abdominal glands of the worker honey bees. Worker bees collect flakes of wax from their abdomen. They then chew these flakes until the wax becomes soft. Subsequently, they are able to mold the wax into cells which essentially form the hive.

Honey bees do not hibernate during cold weather like other species of bee. Instead, they huddle closely together inside the nest, sharing body heat and feeding on food supplies which they have stored up.

Although honey bees are social creatures, they do exhibit some aggressive behavior within the colony. Drones are sometimes evicted from their nests during cold weather; queens will sometimes sting other queens during mating fights for dominance.

Chapter 2 – All About the Honey Bee

The Honey Bee Colony

The honey bee colony can be made up of thousands of bees. It consists of a single queen bee, hundreds of male drones and between 20,000 to 80,000 female worker bees. There are also developing eggs, larvae and pupae.

The season has a huge influence on the size of the honey bee colony. During the active season, a colony could reach up to 80,000 individuals. This is when workers forage for food, store honey for winter and build combs. During the colder seasons, the numbers decline dramatically.

Each type of bee has a different role to play and the population of the colony depends on this social structure. For example, the queen bee is extremely powerful within the colony, but she could not establish new colonies without the help of drones and workers, who provide fertilization, food and wax to build the hive.

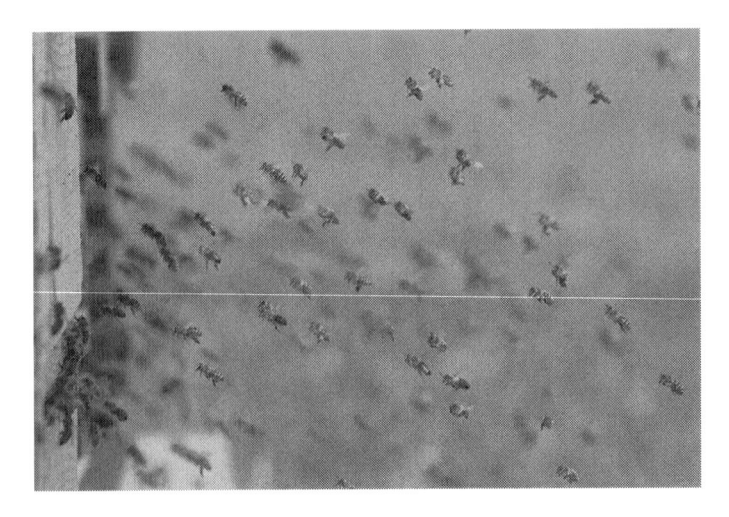

Chapter 2 – All About the Honey Bee

Type of Bees

The colony contains three types of adult honey bees – the queen, male drones and infertile female workers. Within the colony are also eggs, larva, and pupa.

- **The queen** – There is only one egg laying queen in each colony. In contrast there are thousands of worker bees. The queen bee's role is to mate with drones, establish new colonies and lay eggs. Queen bees lay their eggs in the cells of the nest. When the eggs hatch, they become larvae. The queen can produce as many as 2,000 eggs each day.

- **Drones** – these are the male bees. They are the minority within the colony. They have just one role which is to mate with virgin honey bee queens. Once they have mated, the drones die quite quickly.

- **The female worker bees** have several important functions – but they do not produce their own eggs and do not establish new colonies. Young honey bee workers tend the larvae inside the cells. They secrete liquid from their abdominal glands which effectively feeds the larvae with pollen and honey. As they become older, worker bees take responsibility for carrying and storing food which has been gathered by foragers. When fully mature and as strong adults,

Chapter 2 – All About the Honey Bee

their role is to forage for food. They continue doing this until they die.

- **Eggs, Larvae and Pupa** – Every member of the bee colony goes through metamorphosis, starting as egg and then passing through larval and then pupal stages before emerging as adults. The egg is the first stage of metamorphosis. Honey bee larvae (second stage) are essentially legless grubs that consume honey, nectar or pollen. Larvae shed their skin and molt several times prior to entering the pupal stage. This is the third stage of the bee's metamorphosis. After another molt, the pupae will emerge as honey bees and start to carry out their specialized role for the colony. The now mature bees emerge by chewing through the sealed cells.

Swarms

As a honey bee colony develops, swarming becomes inevitable. It basically occurs due to overcrowding within the hive. A swarm is led by an old honey bee queen who leaves the hive. The queen is accompanied by approximately half of the hive's worker bees. A new queen bee will stay in the old hive along with the remainder of the workers.

In a natural environment, honey bees swarm most often in late spring and early summer – during hot times of the day.

Chapter 2 – All About the Honey Bee

Swarming is part of a healthy life cycle of honey bee colonies. However, as a beekeeper, you will aim to reduce the frequency of swarming.

There may be hundreds or thousands of worker bees and a single queen within a swarm. The swarm tends to fly and then rest on shrubs or tree branches. They can rest like this for a few hours or even several days. It depends on weather conditions and how soon a new nesting site can be found. A scout honey bee will look for a new place for the bee colony and as soon as it is found, the swarm fly to their new home.

Although a swarm of bees can look threatening, they will not generally harm people. After all, they do not have any young to defend or a nest to protect. This means that their incentive to sting is much less.

Chapter 3 – How Can We Help Our Bees?

We have seen that there has been a dramatic decline in the numbers of bees populating our planet. Our food production is absolutely dependent on the honey bee.

Become a Beekeeper

Becoming a beekeeper is a wonderful way to try and counteract the deterioration of the honey bee population.

As well as being a highly rewarding and fascinating hobby, you will get to eat your own honey.

Chapter 3 – How Can We Help Our Bees?

In this book, we will guide you through the practicalities of beekeeping and show you that it really is a pastime that you can do.

In addition to beekeeping, there are many other ways that you can support the survival of bees.

Help to Protect Swarms

As discussed in the previous chapter, swarming is a natural phenomenon that occurs when a honey bee colony has reached maximum capacity. The colony then splits in two and a swarm of bees go off in search for a new nest.

In general, honey bees in a swarm look frightening but in reality, are very gentle and are of very little threat.

There is no need to contact pest control. The honey bees will automatically move on quite quickly. However, it may be even more beneficial if you are able to contact a local bee keeper.

They can collect the swarm and take it away. This is good for the beekeeper and can help to save struggling bees. A beekeeper can strengthen the genetic pool on their bee farm by introducing a new swarm of bees.

A swarm that is found, especially in an urban environment, is likely to have come from a feral colony – one living in the wild. It has survived for a substantial period of time in the

Chapter 3 – How Can We Help Our Bees?

wild and has been strong enough to form a swarm – this means that the genetic makeup must be strong.

Without doubt, there is absolutely no reason to contact an exterminator or attempt to spray it with insecticide.

Plant Bee Friendly Plants

Especially in areas where there are few agricultural crops, honey bees depend on flowers growing in your yard for their diet. You can encourage bees to visit your yard by planting single flowering plants and vegetables.

All flowers in the allium family are bee friendly. Bees also like all the mints, beans (except French beans), and flowering herbs. Bees like daisy-shaped flowers – asters and sunflowers, also tall plants such as hollyhock, larkspur and foxgloves. Bees require a lot of pollen and trees are an exceptionally good source of food. Willows and lime trees are very good.

Other good choices include;

- clover
- sage
- oregano
- salvia
- ironweed

Chapter 3 – How Can We Help Our Bees?

- lavender
- yellow hyssop
- alfalfa
- yarrow
- dragonhead
- honeywort
- bee balm
- echinacea
- goldenrod
- buttercup
- English thyme

Also consider flowering trees like sourwoods, oranges, tupelos, and tulip poplars.

Provide a source of shallow water and a secure place where bees can live. Hydration is very important to bees.

Note that feral bees live in everything from underground tunnels to dead trees.

Consider purchasing wooden bee blocks with pre-drilled holes for nesting. Alternatively, provide an amount of loose earth near your water source.

Use only natural and organic pest control methods. A chemical free yard and garden is the perfect place for wild bees to thrive.

Chapter 3 – How Can We Help Our Bees?

Purchase Local Honey

Support beekeepers in your area! This keeps food miles down and helps the beekeeper cover the cost of beekeeping. Local honey complies with all food standards requirements but is not mistreated to give it a longer shelf life.

Buy local honey from venues such as farmer's markets and flea markets. Not only is honey a deliciously sweet treat, there's good evidence to suggest that eating honey produced by bees in your area will help to prevent seasonal allergy attacks. Local honey tends to taste different to 'supermarket' honey – its' flavor is influenced by local plant life and environment.

Bee Friendly

Honey bees only tend to sting if they are provoked. As a beekeeper, you would wear protective clothing. If a bee flies near you when you are not in protective clothing, do not flap your hands. You need to stay calm and move away very slowly (ideally into the shade). The bee will soon lose interest in you.

Chapter 4 – What All Beekeepers Must Know

Chapter 4 – What All Beekeepers Must Know

Beekeeping and the Law

Beekeeping on a small scale can easily be undertaken as a backyard operation, but it's still imperative that you first determine if local zoning laws or other ordinances apply.

If you are a member of a Homeowner's Association, make sure that entity does not prohibit beekeeping.

There are relatively few areas in the U.S. where beekeeping is illegal. However, some areas have laws that put practical constraints on beekeeping. For example, limitations on the number of hives and a requirement that the beekeeper provides water for the bees.

However, most states have "nuisance laws" – these are intended to make illegal activities that most people would object to – such as a barking dog or a strong smell.

Using common sense, think about your neighbors and try not to allow your beekeeping to impact on their daily lives. Sharing a jar or two of honey will surely help! Be sensitive to the fact that people can be fearful of bees, especially if an individual has an allergic reaction to bee stings.

Be prepared to offer educational material to show that your hives will pose no theat. Providing there are nectar and pollen-producing plants, there will be bees in our cities and towns. Indeed, if beekeeping were illegal, you would

Chapter 4 – What All Beekeepers Must Know

simply see more wild bees – the bees would not go away.

It's also important to contact your insurance agent. Find out about additional coverage against accidents. If you can be held accountable for such incidents, extra insurance protection could be a very sound idea.

However, if you do experience objection to your idea of beekeeping – or if there are zoning laws in place to prevent you doing so, you may be able to locate your bees and beehives away from your own yard.

Many beekeepers who are not able to keeps bees at home have arranged to keep their bees on local farms.

Contact local beekeeping associations as they may know a suitable place for you to keep your bees. Also, try contacting fruit and vegetable gardeners, and gardening clubs as they may be able to tell you of a suitable location.

After all, any type of gardener is going to understand the value of pollination.

How Much Time Does Beekeeping Take Up?

Before committing to beekeeping, be sure that you are ready and prepared for the level of dedication required.

The time spent attending to your bees will vary throughout the year. During late Spring and Summer, you will probably spend about an hour a week for the first colony.

Chapter 4 – What All Beekeepers Must Know

Additional colonies will probably take an extra half an hour each. Some weeks you will find it takes more time and some weeks less.

Your time will be spend doing things such as taking protective clothing on and off, lighting a smoker, assembling the kit that you need. This takes time regardless of whether you are looking after one colony or more. Other requirements include extracting and bottling honey and feeding.

During later Fall, Winter and very early Spring, there is very little that actually has to be done. Most beekeepers spend this time to prepare for the following season.

It will take an experienced beekeeper less time. You can expect to get quicker over time.

Chapter 4 – What All Beekeepers Must Know

Scientific Names for Honey Bees

There are four major species of honeybees in the world; Apis Florea (Small Honey Bee), Apis Dorsata (Giant Honey Bee), Apis Cerana (Eastern Honey Bee), and Apis Mellifera (Western Honey Bee). Honey bees that are seen in North America are the Apis Mellifera.

The genus name Apis is Latin for "bee". Mellifera means honey producing. This species is inclined to produce a large quantity of honey for storage over the colder months. So Apis Mellifera basically means pollen collecting and honey producing.

Chapter 4 – What All Beekeepers Must Know

Why Do Bees Sting?

Depending on the role of the bee, there are different uses for their stinging ability. Indeed, the drones (male bees) are incapable of stinging as they do not have stingers. The stinger is a modified ovipositor (egg laying device) so is exclusive to the females.

The worker bees sting as a defensive mechanism to protect their colony. They tend to only sting as a last resort and if they feel under threat.

The honey bee is the only species of bee to die after stinging. When a honey bee stings a person, it cannot pull the barbed stinger back out. This means that it leaves behind not only the stinger, but also part of its abdomen and digestive tract, plus muscles and nerves. This is a massive abdominal rupture that is substantial enough to kill the bee outright.

Queen bees sting for a very different reason to the worker bee. They will sting to eliminate competition within the colony. When a colony of bees becomes 'queen-less', the worker bees begin to raise new queens. Several young queens will emerge simultaneously. They will subsequently fight until only one queen bee remains. They actually use their stinger to kill the other queens.

However, it is extremely rare for a queen bee to sting a person.

Chapter 4 – What All Beekeepers Must Know

How Honey Bees Communicate

Communication between honey bees is fascinating and important for the beekeeper to understand.

There are two main methods employed to aid communication. One is chemical, and the other is choreographic.

Honey Bee Pheromones

All animals produce chemical scents that generate behavioral responses from other members of the same species. These are called pheromones.

The colony is fundamentally dependent on honey bee pheromones. The three types of bee produce numerous pheromones at various times to trigger specific behaviors. Examples include;

- Queen pheromones (known as queen substance) tells the colony that the queen is in residence. This activates many worker bee activities.
- Outside of the hive – the queen pheromones work to attract mates, affecting the behavior of male drone bees.
- At the entrance to the hive, worker bees use pheromones to help guide foraging bees back to their hive. This appealing scent stems from the

Chapter 4 – What All Beekeepers Must Know

'Nassanoff' gland which is at the tip of the worker bee's abdomen.
- Alarm pheromones are used by worker bees to warn of any aggression towards the colony.
- Developing bee larvae and pupae excrete pheromones that allow worker bees to recognize the brood's gender, stage of development and feeding requirements.

Dance of the Honey Bee

To the human observer, the most wonderous language of the honey bee is their unique dance. Communication is accomplished through a series of dances done by foraging worker bees.

They return to the hive with news of nectar, pollen, or water and need to share this information with their fellow worker bees.

The style of dance provides surprisingly accurate information regarding the type of food that the foraging bees have discovered.

Chapter 4 – What All Beekeepers Must Know

Two distinct types of dances can be seen – the 'Round Dance' and the 'Waggle Dance'.

The 'Round Dance' tells other worker bees that there is a food source near the hive (at least within 10 – 80 yards).

The 'Waggle Dance' communicates that the food source was located at a greater distance from the hive. The dance consists of a shivering side to side motion of the abdomen, while the dancing bee forms a figure of eight. The strength of the waggle, the number of times repeated, the direction of the dance, and the sound the bee makes together communicates incredibly detailed information about the location of the food source.

During the dances, the bees pause and offer a sample of the food they have bought back with them. This provides further information about where the food can be found and also what time of flower the food has come from.

Chapter 4 – What All Beekeepers Must Know

What Do Honey Bees Eat?

Honey bees consume pollen and nectar from a variety of flowers which enables the production of honey.

Pollen is a powdery, dusty matter that is produced by various flowering plants. Pollen is an extremely rich and natural food that contains all the nutritional requirements of a honey bee; sugar, carbohydrates, protein, enzymes, vitamins and minerals. Nectar is a sweet liquid that the bees suck out from the flowers. Honey bees collect the nectar and transform it into honey.

Most of the honey bee larvae are fed honey. Larvae that are chosen to become future queens will be fed with royal jelly.

Royal jelly is a white secretion that is generated by mouth glands in young female worker bees. It consists of pollen

Chapter 4 – What All Beekeepers Must Know

and chemicals from the glands of the worker bees. It is extremely rich in proteins and fatty acids.

Workers and drones are fed royal jelly during the first few days of larval development. But future queen larvae consume the royal jelly throughout their entire development.

Since the selected queen honey bee eats a diet of royal jelly, they grow very rapidly and become twice the size of an ordinary honey bee. Thanks to the rich nutritional value of royal jelly, queens can survive for an incredible 3 - 5 years. This compares dramatically to the average life span of the worker and drone bees. The queens are also able to lay up to 2,000 eggs every day.

Lifespan of the Honey Bee

The estimated lifespan of the honeybee varies according to the type of bee.

Queen bees can live up to three years.

Drones have a much shorter lifespan – they either die when they mate – or if they have not mated by the beginning of winter, they are evicted from the colony where they will soon die.

The life expectancy of a worker bee is very dependent on the time of year.

Chapter 4 – What All Beekeepers Must Know

During late spring, summer and early fall, a worker bee can only be expected to live for about 6 weeks. As already illustrated, the purpose of the worker bee is to initially tend to the larvae and pupa (for the initial two weeks) and then to forage for food, collecting nectar and pollen until they die.

Worker bees that are born in the late fall will live longer, as much as 4 – 5 months. This is because they have an additional purpose – to look after the queen and keep her warm during the cold winter season.

Chapter 5 – Exploring the Different Species

Western Honey Bee

Apis mellifera, the European or Western Honey Bee, is the species most widely distributed around the globe and most "domesticated" by man for the cultivation of honey.

Honey bees vary in characteristics such as temperament, disease resistance and productivity. The environment also has a significant impact on a colony of honey bees – for example, honey crops depend on the availability of nearby plants.

The genetic makeup of a colony influences the characteristics of that particular group. This enables beekeepers to select strains in accordance to their priority – pollination, honey crop or bee production.

As a beekeeper, you can consider the traits that characterize specific groups of bees. However, remember that there is a wide variation that exists within stocks. There are always exceptions to the rule.

By making some oversimplifications, beekeepers are better able to understand the different types of bees that are available. There is no 'best' strain of bee – it depends on what individual beekeepers regard as the most important traits for them. This may different to another beekeepers' first choice.

Chapter 5 – Exploring the Different Species

The following subspecies are considered the most popular and are some of the more common commercially available honeybee stocks in the U.S.

European Dark Bee

- *Apis mellifera mellifera;* **the European Dark Bee.** They are sometimes called the German Black Bee or German Dark Bee. This subspecies originated in Europe, stretching from Western Russia through Northern Europe and as far down as the Iberian Peninsula.

    The European Dark Bee was domesticated in Europe and hives were introduced to North American in the 17th Century by early European settlers.

    These are comparatively large for honey bees. They have a stocky body, with plentiful thicker and longer hair. This helps to keep them warm in cooler climates.

    The European Dark Bee is very dark in color. From a distance, they appear to be blackish or a rich dark brown.

    The feral bee population in the U.S. was once dominated by this subspecies. However, new diseases have virtually wiped out the majority of these wild bee colonies.

Chapter 5 – Exploring the Different Species

Positives

A hardy strain that is able to survive in cold winters, even in northern climates.

Low Swarming - making them easier for the beekeeper to manage.

High inclination to collect pollen.

Higher longevity of worker bees and queen. The queens are non-prolific which means that they do not need to be replaced regularly. They can reign over the colony for their entire life and so do not need to be replaced regularly.

Negatives

At present, stock of the German bee is not widely available – this is due to their dramatic decline in numbers worldwide.

Vulnerable to new diseases such as American and European foulbrood.

The German bees, notably the hybrids, can be inclined to exhibit overly defensive behavior. This inevitably makes it a more difficult bee stock for the beekeeper to manage.

Chapter 5 – Exploring the Different Species

Italian Bee

- *Apis mellifera linguistica*; the Italian Honey Bee, is native to Italy and the neighboring Mediterranean. It is sometimes referred to as the Ligurian bee. Introduced to the U.S. in 1859, they very rapidly became the most popular stock in this country – this is still true to the present day.

  This subspecies is the most widely distributed of all honey bees and has proved able to adapt to most climates. However, it has not thrived in humid tropical regions and conversely are less able to cope with cold winters.

  The abdomen has brown and yellow bands. Among the different strains of Italian bees, there exist three different colors; leather; bright yellow (golden); and very pale yellow.

  Their bodies are smaller, and their hair is shorter in comparison to the darker honey bee races.

Positives

Gentle and docile temperament

Prolific breeding

Low tendency to swarm compared to other Western Honey bee races.

Chapter 5 – Exploring the Different Species

Thorough housekeeping and high level of cleanliness. Some scientists regard this as contributing to disease resistance.

Covers the honey with tremendous white 'cappings'.

Fantastic foragers

Generally willing to enter supers

Negatives

Due to their excessive brood rearing, the Italian bees can consume surplus honey in the hive if supers (removable upper sections where the honey is stored) are not removed immediately after the honey flow stops. This is especially notable if they are not able to forage sufficiently

They display a tendency to raid other hives and take the honey, targeting weaker and dead neighboring colonies. This may contribute to the spread of transmittable diseases between hives.

Susceptibility to disease

Chapter 5 – Exploring the Different Species

Carniolan Bee

- *Apis mellifera carnica*; the Carniolan (or Carnies for short) or Grey Honey Bee, or Slovenian Bee.

  This subspecies is indigenous to middle Europe and is smaller than other European bees. It is exceedingly gentle, and colonies build back rapidly as the weather begins to warm in the spring.

  This subspecies is the second most popular among beekeepers and extremely well regarded amongst U.S. beekeepers.

  Positives

  The Carnies are gentle, non-aggressive and docile. This means that they can be kept in populated areas. Beekeepers find that they can be worked with little smoke and protective clothing.

  These bees adjust worker population in accordance to the availability of nectar. Indeed, when nectar becomes readily available in the Spring, the population levels rise extensively and rapidly. Conversely, in cooler weather when nectar is scarce, they swiftly reduce brood production and brood rearing.

  Consequently, they have high worker populations when there are high levels of nectar available. They are therefore able to store large quantities of honey

Chapter 5 – Exploring the Different Species

and pollen during these periods.

The Carniolan bees are also resistant to some diseases and parasites that could destroy colonies of other species.

Less disposed to raiding other colonies and taking their honey. This reduces disease transmission among colonies.

The worker bees tend to live up to 12% longer than other subspecies.

Extremely good builders of wax combs. This can be utilized for products such as candles, soaps, and cosmetics.

Negatives

Carniolan bees have a strong tendency to swarm when a colony becomes overcrowded. This can make them difficult to manage. This may also leave the beekeeper with a very poor honey crop. The beekeeper will need to be enormously vigilant to prevent the loss of swarms.
During very hot summer weather, they tend not to thrive.

The strength of the brood nest tends to particularly depend on the availability of pollen.

As the beekeeper, you make find the dark queen difficult to locate.

Chapter 5 – Exploring the Different Species

Caucasian Bee

- *Apis mellifera caucasica*; the Caucasian Honey Bee.

    Originating in the high valleys of the Central Caucasus. Georgia is the central homeland for the subspecies, but they can also be found in Eastern Turkey, Armenia and Azerbaijan.

    Whilst this stock has been popular in the U.S., its' popularity has diminished over the last few decades.

    The Caucasian Honey Bee is large and moderately colored. It can appear to be gray due to its heavy covering of hair. Some exhibit brown spots.

    The most distinctive characteristic is its exceptionally long tongue – the longest tongue of all breeds. This allows the bees to forage for nectar from flowers that other bee stocks may not be able to reach.

    Positives

    Exceptionally docile and mild natured.

    Enthusiastic brood production resulting in strong colonies. The colony also regulates brood production in accordance to the availability of nectar. Consequently, it has high productivity and great honey yields.

    Good in areas where the highest nectar flow is in mid-summer. This is because colonies reach full

Chapter 5 – Exploring the Different Species

strength in mid-summer

Uses a minimum number of combs to store honey – completely fills up the previous comb before starting a new one. This helps save time when harvesting the honey.

Copes well in cooler, rainy and highly changeable weather.

Negatives

Their gradual spring build up prevents them from producing very large honey crops. They are not well suited to regions where the highest nectar flow is in the spring and early summer.

The enthusiastic use of propolis can make hive management more challenging. It essentially means that frames and hive boxes become significantly stuck together. Propolis is the sticky resin substance (often referred to as bee glue) that is used to seal cracks and joints of bee structures.

Tendency to drift and rob from other hives.

Buckfast Bee

This is a 'manufactured' bee race that resulted from a cross of many strains of bees. The Buckfast was developed by Karl Kehrle (sometimes known as 'Brother Adam'). He was a monk at Buckfast Abbey (Devon, England) where he was responsible for

Chapter 5 – Exploring the Different Species

beekeeping. Bees are still bred there today.

In Great Britain, during the 1920's, bee populations were being destroyed by tracheal mites and thousands of colonies were killed off. Kehrle was tasked with establishing a stock of bees that could survive this deadly disease.

In 1916, there were only 16 surviving colonies in Buckfast Abbey. These consisted of Italian (and of Italian origin), hybrids between Italian and German Black Bee. Kehrle imported some additional Italian queens. The Buckfast Bee is the result of this work.

Positives

Calm behavior and docile temperament, low instinct to sting.

Production of good honey crops.

Strong resistance to disease.

Industrious and enthusiastic foragers.

Low tendency to swarm.

High levels on cleanliness with excellent housekeeping – this helps to reduce the likelihood of disease.

Ability to thrive in cold and wet environments.

Negatives

Chapter 5 – Exploring the Different Species

Restricted amount of brood during the cold seasons.

Where a colony is not re-queened, the Buckfast Bee can become excessively defensive in a second-generation colony.

Spring population build up is moderate. Consequently, they are unable to take full advantage of early nectar flows.

The Russian Bee

This is one of the later stocks to be imported to the U.S. It originated in the Primorsky Krai region of Russia.

During the 1990's, the U.S. saw a massive decline in bee populations due to infestations of parasitic mites. Scientists found that the Russian bees have a distinctive resistance to various parasitic mites. Therefore, the USDA's Honeybee breeding, Genetics and Physiology Laboratory began to use them in breeding programs to improve and strengthen existing stocks.

The USDA ran tests to find out if this stock had evolved resistance to varroa and found that it had. The quarantine phase of this project concluded in 2000. Since that time, bees of this strain have been available commercially.

Chapter 5 – Exploring the Different Species

Genetically, a Russian bee is Caucasian, with some Italian and Carniolan lineage. Despite sharing some of their characteristics, they display their own individual traits.

The Russian bee is dark in color. The abdomen is black, and hair is gray.

Russian bees are disposed to rear brood only during times of nectar and pollen flows. Consequently, brood rearing and colony populations vary according to the environment.

This stock displays some unique behaviors. The colony has queen cells present in their colonies for most of the time. The queens are there to emerge and quickly take over egg laying responsibilities if the queen is lost. They are like an emergency backup queen ready in case things go wrong. In comparison, other stocks rear queens only during times of swarming or queen replacement.

Positives

Gentle temperament with low inclination to sting.

High resistance to disease, including to varroa and the tracheal mite. This may be due in part, to their excellent housekeeping behavior.

Good honey crops.

Negatives

Tendency to swarm – although with proper management, this can be avoided.

Most of the Russian queen bees for sale are hybrid daughters of a breeder queen – the Russian queen openly mated with any drone, which may have come from a variety of stock. The resulting colonies are genetic hybrids. Recent research has revealed the hybrids are only partially resistant to mites. However, research at North Carolina State University has found that even partial resistance is of extreme importance and significance, especially compared with other stocks such as the Italian.

Pure Russian queens can only be guaranteed by isolating the breeding grounds so that the drone stock can also be controlled. This is what happened at the USDA' laboratory.

The Giant Honey Bee

Apis dorsata; the Giant Honey Bee, is found in southern and southeast Asia. The species is highly aggressive when provoked, but is a prolific honey producer. Indigenous peoples in the region routinely harvest honey from the large, exposed combs, but the species has never been formally domesticated.

Chapter 5 – Exploring the Different Species

Africanized Honey Bee

The Africanized Honey Bee, *Apis mellifera scutellata*, also known as the 'killer bee'. With an infamous reputation for extreme aggression, this species, native to central southern Africa, is not any more aggressive than any other species. Its reputation has been vilified as the outcome of breeding experiments in 1956.

In Brazil, genetic scientists were experimenting with breeding a new hybrid that was hoped would yield more honey. The super defensive African bees were crossed with various forms of European bees who had a gentler temperament.

But, unfortunately, some African queen bees escaped into the jungles of Brazil. These queens bred with bees in the jungle and the 'Africanized Honey Bees' became established. These colonies displayed unusual defensive tendencies, keeping guard bees at 20-30 meters from the hive.

When bees were sent out to defend these colonies, the numbers were huge compared to other species, and persistent, traveling long distances in pursuit of the intruder.

The hybrids also showed a tendency to take over existing European bee colonies, which led to further hybridization and rapid reproduction of the new population.

Referred to as the "Africanized" bee, these hybrid strains have spread up through Central America and Mexico and

Chapter 5 – Exploring the Different Species

are now present in the southern United States.

In terms of physical appearance, the Africanized Honey Bee is extremely similar to the much friendlier European Honey Bees. To detect the difference, you would need to do a DNA test or analyze them under a microscope.

It is worth noting that their sting is no more severe, and they do die, after stinging a person.

The crucial difference is their temperament – they are extremely defensive of their hives and react rapidly to any kind of disturbance that is viewed as a threat. As well as chasing an intruder over a long distance, they can remain hyper-defensive for several days after an incident.

Chapter 6 – All About Honey

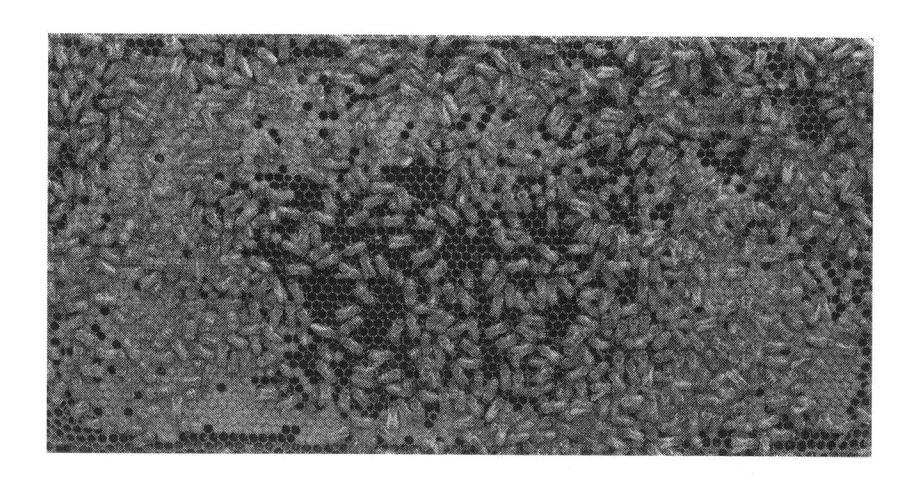

Chapter 6 – All About Honey

How Do Bees Make Honey?

The honey that bees store is an energy "savings account" for leaner (and colder) times of the year. Worker bees go out and collect nectar, which they bring back to the hive where it is converted to honey.

Bees require two different kinds of food. One is honey made from nectar – the sugary liquid that is found in the center of flowers. The other is derived from the anthers of flowers, which contain countless small grains called pollen. Like different colors of flowers, there are also different kinds of pollens.

Honey bees tend to either gather pollen or nectar (not both together). The bee sucks the nectar from the flower and stores it in her special honey stomach. Nectar is comprised of almost 80% water with some complex sugars. Bees have

Chapter 6 – All About Honey

two stomachs – a honey stomach where the honey is stored and their regular stomach. If she is hungry, she will open a valve in the nectar 'sac' and some of the nectar passes through to her own stomach providing her with energy.

The rest she transports back to the 'honey making bees' in the hive when her nectar 'sacs' are full.

The honey stomach holds almost 70mg of nectar and when full, it weighs virtually as much as the bee does. Honey bees need to visit between 100 and 1500 flowers to fill up their honey stomachs.

Nectar is delivered to one of the indoor bees at the hive. These bees suck the nectar from the honey bees' stomach through their mouths. These bees effectively chew the nectar for about half an hour.

During this time, enzymes are breaking down the complex sugars in the nectar and transforming them into simple sugars. This is more digestible for the bees and is less susceptible to bacteria while it is being stored in the hive.

The bees then spread the nectar throughout the honeycombs where water evaporates from it. This turns the nectar into a thicker syrup - this is the turning point where the nectar effectively becomes honey. The bees speed up the drying process by also fanning it with their wings.

Once the honey is the correct consistency – gooey enough - it is placed into storage cells and capped with beeswax. Before beginning another foraging trip, the worker bee combs and cleans herself. This is to ensure that she can

Chapter 6 – All About Honey

work efficiently.

There will be many other worker bees foraging at the same time. It takes approximately 300 bees three weeks to gather 450g of honey. The average hive consists of about 40,000 bees.

Although honey bees can fly at speeds of as much as 15 mph, they are not speed demons. They excel at short trips from flower to flower and must flap their wings as much as 12,000 times a minute to keep their heavy bodies in the air for the return flight to the hive.

Chapter 6 – All About Honey

A single worker bee visits as many as 2,000 flowers a day. A full load of nectar for one trip back to the hive is likely the product of drinking from 50-100 flowers. This level of activity places such a tremendous strain on the workers that they live only three weeks on average.

To gain some perspective on the incredible cooperative effort that goes into the production of honey in a hive, one worker bee will never produce more than 1/12th of a teaspoon of honey in his whole life!

But an entire colony, which can be made up of as many as 60,000 bees, has the potential to produce as much as 200 lbs. / 90.72 kg of honey per year. Now that is one heck of an assembly line at work!

Honey bees make vast quantities of honey to feed the entire colony in the summer and to store enough food in the winter.

Why Do Bees Make Honey?

Honey bees are unique in that they overwinter as a colony. This is the main difference between honey bees and other types of bees. The storage of food, in the form of honey, is what enables to the honey bee to survive the winter and maintain the colony.

This compares to bumble bees who make a small colony of only about 100 bees. They do collect nectar and pollen just

Chapter 6 – All About Honey

like honey bees and they store excess pollen and nectar (which they turn into honey) within a small colonial nest.

However, bumble bees do not make a big comb filled with honey and they do not cluster like honey bees. They tend to let the nest decline and die out in the autumn.

Only the new pregnant bumble bee queen will survive the winter (either hibernating alone or a few together). In the spring, each queen will begin to make a new nest from scratch – with only herself as the only egg layer and foraging on her own in the very early days of the new nest.

This means that there is no need for the enormous over wintering store of honey.

The honey bee colony does not hibernate but stays active and clusters together to stay warm during the winter. This requires a lot of food, hence the massive gathering and storing of honey throughout the spring and summer.

Although a colony only needs approximately 20 – 30 lbs. of honey to survive the average winter, the bees tend to collect much more if they have adequate storage space. This is ideal for the beekeeper.

Bees have been using the same methods to create honey for the last one hundred and fifty million years.

Chapter 6 – All About Honey

Beeswax

The youngest bees cluster in large numbers to increase their body temperatures. Eight paired glands on the underside of the worker bees' abdomen produces tiny slivers of wax. These droplets of wax harden into flakes when exposed to the air. The wax is discarded in or at the hive.

The workers take the flakes into their mouths and soften them into the workable material they use to construct the honeycomb.

The hive worker bees collect up the beeswax and use it to form cells for honey storage and larval and pupal protection within the beehive. Indeed, the comb in which honey is stored is comprised of hexagonal cells built of beeswax. It is in these chambers that the bees also brood. For the wax-making bees to secrete wax, the optimum

Chapter 6 – All About Honey

temperature in the hive is between 33 and 36 degrees Celsius.

When beeswax is new, it is light yellow. In time, it darkens to a rich gold and finally becomes brown. Chemically, beeswax is comprised of asters of fatty acids and various long-chain alcohols.

Beeswax has many uses, from traditional candle making, to an ingredient in lip balms and even as a coating for some medicine.

Beeswax is also well used in the food industry. For example, it is used as a glazing agent (to prevent water loss or used to protect the surface of some fruits). It is used as an outer layer for cheese; it provides a seal that is perfectly airtight, this prevents mold growth. It is also used as a sweetener and natural chewing gum often utilizes beeswax.

It is also used in the making of electrical components and is an ingredient in some types of varnish.

Beeswax is edible although, for humans, it is of very low nutritional value – this is because we find it difficult to digest. Some birds can digest beeswax (such as honeyguides) and beeswax is the main component of a wax moth larvae's diet.

Best estimates for top-producing hives place beeswax production at 24-30 lbs. / 11-14 kg of beeswax per 1 lb. / 0.45 of honey.

Chapter 6 – All About Honey

How Much Honey?

One colony of honey bees can produce more than 60 lbs. (27 kg of honey) in a good season. However, an average hive would generate around 25 lbs. (11 kg) of surplus honey.

Bees fly an incredible 55,000 miles to make just one pound of honey. That is equivalent to 2.2 times around the world.

A strong colony will produce 2 – 3 times more honey than they require. This means that the bees do not miss the honey that is taken by the beekeeper.

During the autumn, the beekeeper may feed the bees sugar syrup. This is not always necessary but supplements any loss caused by the beekeeper taking the honey.

Different Types of Honey

There are various types of honey – some is clear and runny and other types are opaque and hard. The type of foliage and flowers available to the bees affects the type of honey they can make.

Crops such as oil seed rape produce large quantities of honey that sets very hard – so hard that the bees cannot use it during the cold weather. Garden flowers tend to result in a clear liquid honey.

Chapter 6 – All About Honey

If the beekeeper locates the beehive out of the range of a variety of floral sources, the bees will create a monofloral honey.

Examples of monofloral honey include pure clover, orange blossom. This can be difficult to achieve – most beekeepers produce honey that is the result of a mixture of floral sources.

Chapter 7 – A History of Beekeeping

The relationship between man and the honey bee was based first on simple thievery on the part of humans. When a hive was found in a tree or a cave, it was opportunistically raided for its honey.

Because such extractions happened only sporadically, the sweet stuff was regarded as a rare, luxury item.

In time, this random practice evolved to the actual cultivation of bees. The insects were raised in boxes, a solution that made honey more readily available.

However, for the honey to be safely harvested, the bees had to be killed with sulfur fumes. Attempts to take the honey by any other method enraged the insects and created great danger for the beekeeper.

Gum Hives

In the Eastern and Southeastern United States, in the 19th century, hollow sections of the black gum trees were set up in apiaries. This marks the very beginning of beekeeping.

These hives were known as 'gums' (named after the black gum trees from which they were made). Occasionally, some beekeepers place small sticks over the open top of the hive – this helped to provide support for honeycomb construction.

Chapter 7 – A History of Beekeeping

Until the 20th century, this basic form of beekeeping continued. It relied on an extremely destructive technique; the hive and colony were destroyed so that honey could be harvested. Very often, the bees were also eliminated using burning sulfur.

Bee gum hives are still used in the United States today. However, with significant changes to hive maintenance and honey harvesting. In central Europe, commercial beehives were also constructed from hollowed out tree trunks. But the European version used removable bars that were placed on top of the open trunk.

The bars were not simply used as an aid to honeycomb construction – but also enabled removal of individual honeycombs without destroying the colony and hive.

Early Beehive Designs

There existed some hives in the 1800's that used well thought out designs. These discouraged the queens from laying eggs in some parts of the hive. This meant that honey could be harvested without damaging the entire colony.

These beekeepers realized that the queens were not inclined to lay her eggs in more than one area in the hive – so they constructed side and top compartments with passageways for the bees.

Chapter 7 – A History of Beekeeping

The hives often had a place for the brood nest in the center and compartments for honey storage on the sides. This worked as a queen excluder. There was no physical barrier, but the design simply relied on the natural behavior of the bees.

During the 1800's, some skep hives (constructed from grass straw) and box hives (simple shelters) had a second container (or 'super') for the bees to store their honey.

Supers were sometimes put on top of log sections to allow for easy honey harvesting.

Although the use of supers allowed the beekeeper to remove honey without destroying the colony, it was difficult for the beekeeper to check on the bees. The beekeeper would not know if there was a problem with disease, if there was no queen, or if the bees were starving. Indeed, the beekeeper could not inspect each comb.

Movable Comb Hives

Beekeepers recognized, for a long time prior, that bees tended to build their honeycombs about 1 and 3/8 inches apart. Some beekeepers built hives that encouraged the bees to build combs along 'top bars' that were spaced about 1 and 3/8 inches apart.

Chapter 7 – A History of Beekeeping

These 'top bars' enabled beekeepers to carefully remove combs for inspection without damaging them. These became known as movable comb hives.

With a movable comb hives, beekeepers could start a new colony by dividing a hive. The beekeeper could also inspect the health of the bees, locate the queen, and even cut honeycomb without destroying the brood nest.

Bees in movable comb colonies were disturbed much less than bees in fixed-comb hives. This meant, thankfully, that the bees experienced less stress as a result and consequently that beekeepers were subjected to much reduced stinging.

Numerous comb hive designs used 'frames' for the bees to build their combs inside.

In 1789 in Switzerland, François Huber, developed a hive with a fully movable frame known as the "Leaf Hive." The frames touched and formed a box, but could be individually examined as if turning the pages in a book.

Huber has been credited with inventing the first movable frame hive.

This design inspired in part the work of an American beekeeper, the Rev. Lorenzo Lorraine Langstroth, who is popularly considered to be the "Father of American Beekeeping."

Chapter 7 – A History of Beekeeping

The Work of L.L. Langstroth

In 1848, while serving as the principal of a Philadelphia girls' school, L.L. Langstroth took up beekeeping to cope with his long bouts of depression. In 1860, in his book *Langstroth on the Honey-Bee*, he acknowledged the importance of Huber's Leaf Hive in his methodology.

> "The use of the Huber hive had satisfied me that, with proper precautions, the combs might be removed without enraging the bees, and that these insects were capable of being tamed to a surprising degree. Without knowledge of these facts, I should have regarded a hive permitting the removal of the combs as quite too dangerous for practical use."

The beehive that Langstroth patented in October 1852, is still the standard used in many parts of the world today.

The bees build their honeycomb in movable frames. These are designed so that the bees cannot attach the comb to adjacent frames or to the walls of the hive. The arrangement allows for numerous advantages:

- The frame can be removed without cutting the comb, thus allowing it to be used and filled again.
- Colonies can be multiplied more rapidly.
- Weak colonies can be strengthened, and a new queen introduced more easily.
- Hives can be checked regularly for problems, like

parasites, which can be corrected.
- Hives can be stacked with the queen kept at a lower level, maximizing honey production and ease of handling at the upper levels.

Langstroth's innovations allowed for honey to be produced in a more cost-effective way and at a larger scale. Surplus honey is removed without killing the bees, and the comb is then re-used to make additional honey.

All of Langstroth's practical advice on managing bee hives is contained in this 1853 work, *The Hive and the Honey-Bee*, which is still in print today.

Mass Production by A.I. Root

Unfortunately, Langstroth's mental health was not good. He developed a complete preoccupation with the patent process and was adamant that he retained all rights to the production of his designs.

It was not until Amos Ives Root, a jewelry manufacturer in Medina, Ohio, began to produce the hives in 1869 that raising bees via this method became widespread.

Root saw the benefits of Langstroth's design and rapidly became the largest maker of beekeeping equipment in the world. Aspects of his company are still in business today, including Root Candles of Medina, Ohio.

By opting to sell the hives disassembled, Root was able to lower his production costs. This and the availability of rail

Chapter 7 – A History of Beekeeping

transport led to the broad adoption of the Langstroth hives by beekeepers. At the peak of Root's business, his company was shipping four freight cars of beekeeping equipment a day.

Modern Beekeeping

After a century and a half of novices being faced with assembling their own hives as an accepted part of the practice of keeping bees, pre-assembled and painted hives are now readily available.

It is a reality of modern life that fewer people have either the necessary tools or workspace to build their hives, but this should not be a detriment to keeping bees. You can borrow tools, or acquire them quite inexpensively at most hardware store.

Chapter 7 – A History of Beekeeping

As a beginner, start with a couple of hives with eight frames only. Each of the boxes will weigh approximately 30 lbs. / 14 kg when full.

This small-scale operation allows the novice to learn the ropes and to become accustomed to caring for and lifting the boxes without excessive physical strain — or excessive amounts of honey produced.

Remember that it's always possible to expand your hives. The bees are more than willing to help with that process!

You have a lot to learn, so don't overwhelm yourself just as you're starting out. This is a process much like planning a garden. You must first select a location and consider the amount of sun, shade, and water available for your bees.

Consider a calendar of harvest dates, a way to use or preserve the honey, your bees produce, and what needs to be done to get ready for the off-season.

Chapter 8 - Placing Your Hives

Chapter 8 - Placing Your Hives

Locating the Perfect Place

It may surprise you to discover that bees can be kept in a variety of settings, including an urban rooftop. The industrious insects will travel for miles to forage for the food they need, and they are highly adaptable.

There are basic guidelines to follow in selecting a site that will work for both you and your bees, regardless of your current place of residence.

Chapter 8 - Placing Your Hives

Do not purchase your equipment and bees until you have chosen a site for the hives, assured your free access to the area, and made sure that no legal restrictions apply.

You want everything planned and in place before you begin to work with a package of live bees.

Seek 'Light Shade'

In considering locations to place your hives, look for an area that offers some degree of protection against the afternoon sun, but that is not fully shaded. Light or "dappled" shade will make working with the bees more comfortable for you.

In general, the more sun exposure the hives receive, the more resistant they are to various invasive pests. Direct or full sun, however, will cause the internal temperature of the hive to heat up, requiring the colony to work harder to regulate heat levels.

On the other hand, deep shade promotes dampness and creates a listless hive.

Also, try to pick a spot with minimal wind, but that still offers good ventilation. If necessary, plant or build a windbreak at the back of the hives to shut out harsh winter winds that will cause stress to your colony.

Tall shrubs work for this purpose or you can hang a burlap barrier between a series of fence posts.

Chapter 8 - Placing Your Hives

Dry, Level Ground

Place the hives facing to the southeast on dry, level ground well away from other animals and livestock and safe from vandals.

In positioning the actual stands, however, make sure that the front of the hive is about an inch lower than the rear. This allows rainwater to drain out.

Ensure that you have adequate space to move around the perimeter of all your boxes, especially at the rear of the box where the beekeeper spends most of the time working.

Keep the hives at a good distance from residences and areas where children are playing, including swimming pools.

Although bees are not naturally aggressive, curious children can be seriously injured if they begin investigating your colony and accidentally agitate your bees.

Water and Vegetation

A year-round water source is absolutely critical! When bees are foraging, they collect water to dilute their honey and to help cool the hive.

Bees will seek out the nearest source of water, so especially in a populated area make sure that you provide them with water close by to keep them well away from the neighbors.

Think about using an outdoor faucet that can drip slowly.

Chapter 8 - Placing Your Hives

This would provide adequate moisture for your bees; or you can set out pie pans filled with gravel and topped off with water.

There is no need for anything elaborate, but a constant supply is required. (I'll discuss more about watering techniques later in this text.)

The area should offer ample stores of nectar and pollen for the entire summer season, but don't allow weeds and other vegetation to block the entrance to the hives. Overgrowth will cut down on ventilation and create more work for the bees coming in and out of the box.

If possible, install some sort of weed barrier to keep the work area clear. This is preferable to mowing, since you don't want grass clippings to get into the front door of the colony. Barrier options include gravel, bark mulch, or patio pavers.

Convenient Access

Ideally, your bee yard will be on your own property or adjacent to your home, so you will have complete access to your tools and equipment. It's especially convenient if these items can all be stored in a waterproof shed or container adjacent to the yard.

If you cannot keep your bees in your backyard or on your own property, be sure to choose a location that allows you to park nearby with room to turn around.

Chapter 8 - Placing Your Hives

Access should be easy and safe throughout the entire year, not just during the summer.

If you decide that you may be able to use land belonging to someone else, go into the conversation prepared. Provide personal references to illustrate your character, and be ready to explain what is involved in keeping bees. Expect to pay a small rental fee or offer to split the season's honey production with the landowner.

Explain the seasonal schedule you will be keeping and the times when you would be on the property. Describe your vehicle, and discuss matters like security and liability.

If the landowner suggests an alternate location that is not suitable for bees, politely explain why you can't use that site, thank the person for their time, and move on.

Although it's common for beekeepers to opt to put bees where they *can* rather than in the most desirable location, try to discipline yourself to selecting a site that is good for all concerned — you, your bees, and the landowner.

Chapter 8 - Placing Your Hives

Urban Beekeeping

There are laws regulating honey bees and beekeeping in virtually all urban areas across the United States.

State laws and regulations are designed, first and foremost, to control bee diseases. In general, they tend to regulate movement and entry of bees; issue permits and certificates; control apiary location; and are responsible for quarantine, inspection and methods of treating diseased colonies.

Make sure you are aware of all beekeeping regulations before starting out. You and your bees will appreciate getting set up correctly - any future change will be very disruptive to both you and the colony.

Be aware that you may have to pay fees. Also, it is very likely that your equipment and hives will be inspected. In cases where you do not own the property / land, ensure

Chapter 8 - Placing Your Hives

that you have the building owner's permission before setting up your hives.

Urban hives also need to be protected from the wind, to have partial shade, and to be adjacent to a water supply. If your hives will be placed on the roof of a building, light-topped roofs are preferable to black-tops where temperatures can exceed 120 degrees F.

Make sure all individuals with access to the roof are informed about the presence of the hives; and take proper steps and precautions to secure the boxes against tampering — for the sake of all concerned. If possible, limit the proximity in which people may approach the hives to lessen the chance of painful stings and any disturbance (accidental or otherwise) to the hive.

Chapter 9 – Beekeepers at Work

Beekeeping husbandry practices are not difficult to learn, although there are many opinions about the "right" methods.

Most people who take up apiculture as a hobby or vocation don't have a fear of the bees themselves.

Still, even the most confident novice finds their first encounter with a working hive a little daunting in terms of numbers and sound.

It's difficult not to have initial apprehension at the sound of thousands of buzzing bees or the sight of a frame crawling alive with the industrious insects.

The Beekeeping Community

Chapter 9 – Beekeepers at Work

Making friends with an experienced beekeeper is an excellent way to serve as a kind of apprenticeship. Another truly fantastic opportunity is to join a local beekeeping club if possible.

It's an incredibly precious and invaluable learning experience to spend time with an experienced beekeeper as they tend a hive; witness the quiet and truly peaceful rhythm of the work.

In conversation with an experienced apiarist, you will learn years of insights into bee husbandry and in direct relation to the chore at hand. There's no substitute for that kind of learning.

This is not to say you can't learn basic beekeeping from a book. If I thought that was the case, I'd hardly be spending my time writing the volume you're currently holding in your hands.

Another beneficial way to learn more is through YouTube. Like all enthusiasts of any hobby, beekeepers love to talk about what they do, and they love to share videos online. YouTube is a veritable treasure trove of visual information.

It can help you to get an idea of how beekeepers work – there are authentic videos of beekeepers at work, showing techniques and sharing tips.

Chapter 9 – Beekeepers at Work

Your First Beehives

It is very advantageous to start out with two hives. This gives you the ability to 'compare and contrast' normal and abnormal events in each one. Also, with two hives, the chances are much higher that at least one of your colonies will survive the winter. Indeed, the death of a solo colony during the cold months can be a huge disappointment since you'll be forced to start from scratch in the spring.

It's completely normal for a new beekeeper's first-year honey harvest to be small.

As you shop for your first hives, remember that commercial boxes are outfitted with 10 frames. Most home beekeepers, however, tend to prefer to work with 8-9 frames. This is in consideration of the weight involved and to reduce the number of bees killed when frames are removed for inspection and then re-inserted in the boxes.

Eight frames boxes are available for purchase, or you can buy 10 frame units and limit the number of frames you place. Regardless, understand that weight will be a primary consideration. When a ten-frame box is completely full of honey, it may weigh as much as 60 lbs. / 27.21 kg.

In any box arrangement, the two frames on the outside are dummies, known as "follower boards." These create an airspace on the sides of the box to act as insulation against heat and cold.

So, in a 10-frame box filled up to capacity, your bees will be filling 8 frames in any given box with honeycomb.

Chapter 9 – Beekeepers at Work

As you become more experienced with your own hives and get a working sense of their capacity, you will be able to make informed decisions about the number of frames with which you want to work.

Buying Hive Kits

For the beginner, a complete beehive kit is an economical way to get started. It also ensures you have all the parts required for a properly functioning colony. Hives are built of either white pine or red cedar.

The latter is an excellent choice for its durability, light weight, and superior insulating qualities. Indeed, red cedar wood is naturally resistant to rot. On the downside, the material is more expensive than pine.

Eight-frame boxes measure:

- 13.75 inches / 34.93 cm wide
- 20 inches / 50.8 cm long
- 9.5 inches / 24.13 cm deep

Standard Langstroth frames are 9 1/8 inches / 23.2 cm deep. (Frames included in kits may or may not come with the wax foundation material. Always check and order the foundation as well if necessary.)

An eight-frame, red cedar, beehive kit with a screen bottom that includes two deeps (brood boxes), the outer and inner covers, the hive floor, and the necessary hardware for

Chapter 9 – Beekeepers at Work

assembly sells for $225-$250 / £144-£160.

Estimated assembly time with frames is 1.5 hours using a drill or appropriate screwdriver.

Note that this package does not include other hive components discussed below, including queen excluders, honey supers, and top feeders.

Chapter 9 – Beekeepers at Work

Where additional pieces of equipment are mentioned, I'll provide approximate prices. Also, the configuration of beginner kits varies widely by supply house. In this regard, the Internet is the beekeeper's friend, allowing for ease of 'comparison' shopping.

All the materials in a beginner's hive kit are in addition to the tools you will need to work with your bees. For example, protective clothing, smoker. Such items will be covered in the following section.

To Paint or Not to Paint?

Hives made of less expensive lumber, like soft pine, are inclined to weather and rot quickly. For this reason, they do need to be protected with a coat of paint. Although it's common for hives to be painted white, the bees don't really have a preference!

In fact, bees are so intelligent, if you paint your hives different colors, each colony of bees will quickly learn which home they belong to and go unerringly to the "right" hive.

However, the choice of white for hives does have a practical justification. The light color reflects heat away from the hive during the hot months. If you live in a colder climate, however, a darker color that will absorb and hold heat may be a better option.

Talk to experienced beekeepers in your area if you are uncertain on color choice relative to climate. Beyond that,

Chapter 9 – Beekeepers at Work

it's a simple paint job.

Two coats will be sufficient, and remember to only paint the outside of the hive. This includes leaving the top and bottom edges of the boxes unpainted.

Be sure to do this job well in advance of hiving your bees to minimize their exposure to toxic chemical fumes.

Creating Your Bee Yard

Although you can put your hives directly on the ground, using a simple wooden pallet to achieve a little elevation is the better option. This will cut down on the chance of wood rot and improve overall air circulation as well as prevent the hive from flooding during heavy rain.

Also, if you are a beginner on a budget, you may be able to find a couple of pallets for free. Not everything in your bee yard must come out of a catalog or be ordered from a fancy beekeeping outlet to be functional.

Other options include putting bricks down to create a working surface and then elevating your hives on cinder blocks or some other kind of raised stand.

Always consider the potential for predators. Depending on the area where you live, likely suspects for honey thievery range from bears on down to skunks and raccoons. Skunks don't just go after the honey, but will stir up the bees and then eat them like they're candy!

Chapter 9 – Beekeepers at Work

To mitigate this kind of destruction, your hives need to sit at least 18 inches off the ground. Fortuitously, this will also place them at a more convenient working height for you.

Over the winter, beekeepers face potential damage from mice that come into the hive and use it as a warm place to wait out the cold months.

Although the mice don't harm the bees, they can do substantial damage to the frames and boxes, chewing through the foundation material and destroying the wood.

Always choose level, dry ground to place your hives. It is extremely important to guarantee that nothing gets in the way of your bees being able to fly freely in and out of their home.

Working from the Bottom Up

Hive bottom boards come in both solid and screened formats. Screen boards can assist with airflow. Additionally, hive debris can simply fall out and onto the ground.

Bees are extremely clean. They take "cleansing flights" out of the hive rather than defecate inside - unless they're suffering from some type of illness.

After the bottom board is in place, two brood boxes or deeps are stacked on top of it. Although these boxes will be checked to ensure the health of the bees and to monitor the condition of the brood, no honey is harvested from them. Any honey stored in the deeps is reserved for the bees

Chapter 9 – Beekeepers at Work

themselves to help them survive the winter.

The frames are designed to fit vertically in slots built into the boxes. Frames consist of a wooden border around a foundation material on which the bees will directly build their honeycomb. Most beekeepers use wax foundation material, although plastic is also an option.

The frames are arranged in the boxes at the correct distance. This helps create the "bee space" which prevents the honeycomb from being built across more than one section.

This is the arrangement that allows for the frames to be removed and the honey extracted without destroying the honeycomb. The frames are then returned to the hive, so the bees can use the empty cells again.

The length of time you will work with your bees before you can begin to harvest your own honey varies by location. Simply keep a watch on the capacity of the lower brood box and the upper "deep."

When the upper box is filled to 85% capacity with honey, you are ready to put a queen excluder in place. This keeps the queen in the lower boxes, but allows the worker bees to pass back and forth easily.

Then you can put a honey "super" on top of the brood box. The honey super is roughly half as deep as the brood boxes. Add one super at a time. Don't put the second one in place until the first one is about half full.
The inner cover is placed on top of the last super to create an insulating dead air space, with the hive's roof going on

Chapter 9 – Beekeepers at Work

top of that. The roof telescopes to cover the entire structure and has an overhanging edge that protects the hive from rainwater. Covers lift cleanly away, and thus may need to be weighted down so they don't blow off.

(Obviously the inner cover and roof sit on top of the brood boxes initially and then are moved up when the supers are added.)

Hive Tools

The bees will effectively glue the inner cover down with an excreted material called propolis. This is a reddish-brown substance much like resin.

The bees take sap and mix it with their own discharge and with beeswax to create the propolis. This they then use to coat their hives.

Beekeepers use a prying tool or frame lifter to free sections of the hive for examination. Most hive tools have a flat, prying end and a hooked lifting end. The cost for hive tools falls in the range of $5-$10 / £3-£6.

Chapter 9 – Beekeepers at Work

Entrance Reducer

When you are setting up a hive with a new package of bees, put an entrance reducer in place. This piece fits across the front of the hive's base and is a simple notched piece of wood.

Remember that new hives are comprised of a relatively small number of bees.

By giving the insects a smaller entrance, they will more effectively be able to defend their home until their numbers grow.

Entrance reducers are also a good way to discourage mice from entering the hive.
As the colony grows, you can enlarge the entrance and

Chapter 9 – Beekeepers at Work

ultimately remove the reducer all together (during the summer). In preparation for winter, you can put the entrance reducer back in position.

At the height of summer, a working colony may have as many as 60,000 bees, with the population falling to around 5,000 during the winter.

Chapter 10 – Introducing the Bees to Your Hive

When it is time to introduce these industrious creatures to their new home, they will immediately get to work tending their queen and storing honey. It is of critical importance that everything is ready before introducing the bees.

Buying a Package of Bees

Introducing a colony of bees to their new home is a process called hiving. It is accomplished by purchasing and introducing an artificial swarm of bees, called a package, to the hive.

A typical package weighs 3 lbs. / 1.36 kg. It will contain a single queen marked with a dot for ease of identification. (There is also an option to purchase queens with clipped wings.)

The queen is placed in her own tiny cage. This is so the other bees can get used to her smell and accept her. If they were to see her as an intruder, she would be killed.

The package is a wooden box with screen sides. In the upper center, a can of syrup is placed in a central hole to provide a source of nutrition for the bees during transit.

Purchase your bees from a supplier that guarantees their bees to be mite free. Depending on location, the bees may be sent by postal mail or through a commercial overnight

Chapter 10 – Introducing the Bees to Your Hive

or second-day carrier.

Shipping costs vary, but typically the packages themselves start at around $150 / £96. Costs may be reduced if you can visit the apiary and pick up the bees yourself.

The Arrival of Your Bees

As soon as you have the package, check that the bees are alive. If you find that there is an inch or more of dead bees at the bottom, contact the supplier immediately. This is an alarming indication that there may be a problem with these bees.

On their arrival, put your bee package in a cool, dark place to allow them a little time to calm down. Make sure this area is draft free.

Lightly mist the outside of the package screen – use a spray bottle with sugar syrup to feed the bees. This will help the bees feel more relaxed prior to unboxing or "hiving" the package.

Ensure that the spray bottle you use for the sugar syrup is completely clean and uncontaminated. It must not ever have been used for pesticides or cleaning solutions.

Fill it with 1:1 sugar syrup. This should consist of 1-part white cane sugar dissolved in 1-part warm water (by weight or volume) and cooled down to room temperature.

The optimum time to install bees into their new hive is late afternoon. Ensure that your smoker is well lit. It is unusual

Chapter 10 – Introducing the Bees to Your Hive

to require the smoker while installing bees, but it is very good practice to have it ready at all times while inspecting bees.

Handling the Queen Cage

First, remove one of the frames from your brood box and slide a rubber band over it to hold the queen cage in place inside the hive. You will also need a small marshmallow and a medium-sized screw.

Remove the queen cage from the package by lifting out the can of syrup. Slide the queen cage out of the box being careful not to drop it inside, and cover the hole in the package by just setting the can of syrup on top.

If there are any bees adhered to the queen cage, use a handful of grass to gently brush them away. Since bees do not attack plants, this will not upset the insects.
The queen is held in her tiny cage with a cork. Use the screw exactly as you would a corkscrew to remove the cork.

Wait until the queen is looking the other way. Then pull the cork. Cover the hole and again, when she is looking the other way, plug the hole with the marshmallow.

Place the queen cage under the rubber band and put the frame in the middle of the hive.

Chapter 10 – Introducing the Bees to Your Hive

Releasing the Bees

For new beekeepers, the easiest way to release the bees is to take out enough frames to allow the package to sit inside the brood box. Remove the syrup can and put the inner top on the brood box.

Punch some additional holes in the syrup can and turn it upside down over the opening in the center of the inner. This will allow the bees to suck down the syrup.

More experienced beekeepers will knock all the bees in the package down to the bottom of the shipping box; remove the feeding can; and then dump the bees into the brood box. This will, however, agitate the bees and can be a very daunting project for a first-timer to attempt alone.

Chapter 10 – Introducing the Bees to Your Hive

For this reason, the slower, more conservative approach to hiving is recommended until you are completely comfortable working with your bees and have gotten past your natural reticence about getting stung.

Installing a Hive Top Feeder

Over the course of a day or two, the bees will empty the syrup can and then it will be time to provide them with a hive top feeder filled with a 50/50 mixture of water and granulated sugar.

Hive top feeders are polystyrene trays that fit directly on top of the brood box and under the hive "roof." The inner cover isn't put in place while a hive top feeder is in use.

There are numerous advantages to using a feeder of this nature.

- The bees can eat without the hive being left open.
- The hive does not have to be opened completely for the feeder to be re-filled.
- The arrangement minimizes the degree to which the new colony is disturbed.

A typical hive top feeder holds around 3 gallons / 11.35 liters and retails for $25-$30 / £16-19

Sugar water is offered to bees anytime the available supplies of pollen are low or nonexistent. This is also an excellent method for medicating your bees if necessary since medicines can be dissolved in the water – as well as

Chapter 10 – Introducing the Bees to Your Hive

the sugar content.

To further stimulate feeding behavior, some beekeepers also install a pollen substitute packet or "protein patty" directly on top of the frames (along with the use of a hive top feeder).

Each protein patty weighs approximately 1 lb. / 0.45 kg and packs are typically comprised of 10 patties at a cost of $20-$25 / £13-£16.

Hydration for Your Bees

Bees need access to safe water sources near the hive.

Note that they risk drowning by trying to drink from birdbaths; birds, fish, frogs and other wildlife are a threat to bees at river and lakes.

One option is to place pans / bowls with rocks or marbles at the bottom – and then fill with water. The rocks or marbles act as a place for the bee to land while they have a drink. This minimizes the risk of accidental drowning.

Checking the Queen Release

When you install the hive top feeder, use this time to also ensure that the queen has been successfully released from her tiny cage.
Remove the top hive cover and examine the queen cage.

Chapter 10 – Introducing the Bees to Your Hive

The marshmallow should have been eaten through so that the cage is empty.

Now is the time to remove the package box and the queen cage - plus install the remaining frames. Place the frames with extreme care to reduce risk of killing any of your bees.

Leave the hive alone for a week. After that length of time, the bees should be producing honeycomb and actively collecting pollen. Continue to feed them until the first brood box is filled with honey and then you are ready to add the second box.

Expect the bees to consume as much as a quart / 0.94 liter of syrup per day. When they are new to a hive, bees load up on syrup. This stimulates their wax cells, so they will start building comb.

Protective Clothing

As a beekeeper, you will require a protective ventilated suit and jackets; hat and tie down veil; and gloves. This well designed protective clothing guards against stings while working with your bees. Often the degree to which a beekeeper "suits up" is in direct proportion to their level of confidence and experience.

- jacket $75-$100 / £48-£64
- full suit $100-$150 / £64-£96
- hat / veil combos $50-$75 / £32-£48
- gloves $25-$50 / £16-£32

Chapter 11 - Inspecting Your Hives

Hive inspections allow beekeepers to monitor the health of their bees and to get an idea of the productivity of the colony. As you will see in subsequent sections, there are fairly set times or conditions when a beekeeper needs to open the hive and check for signs of progress.

The Bee Smoker

The bee smoker is vital during hive inspections. The purpose is to keep the bees calm while you tend to the hive. The smoke masks the insects' alarm pheromones and disrupts their ability to communicate. Consequently, defensive aggression is kept to a minimum.

Using paper and kindling to build a bed of embers, light the smoker and then add some fuel. Popular choices include:

- burlap
- corrugated cardboard
- egg cartons

Some beekeepers use a fabric called hessian. This ignites easily and produces optimum amounts of smoke.

Chapter 11 - Inspecting Your Hives

The fuel is contained in a can and the smoke is dispensed through a spout at the front. Bellows at the back of the smoker channel the cool, white smoke out of the spout and feed the embers inside the can with air.

The price for a bee smoker falls in a range of $25-$50 / £16-£32.

Performing an Inspection

First off, suit up and light your smoker. When you have a good flow of cool, white smoke, direct a stream at the entrance to the hive. This will help to calm down the guard bees situated at the opening.

Next, remove the hive roof. Blow a few puffs of smoke around the edges. Then, take off the top cover. Direct more smoke at the frames to drive the bees lower into the hive.

Chapter 11 - Inspecting Your Hives

Using your hive tool, loosen the frames. These will be glued in place with some amount of propolis. Take out the first dummy board and set it aside before moving onto the first frame.

On the initial inspection, look for evidence that the queen is actively laying eggs. There should be larvae visibly curled up in cells of the honey comb, or some cells will be capped off with a light tan wax. Such cells are called "brood".

When brood begins to hatch, a colony may expand by as many as 2,000 bees per day. An active queen deposits one egg every 10 seconds and lays up to 1.5 million eggs during her lifetime.

Both pollen and clear nectar will also be present. Colors vary depending on the type of plants on which the bees are feeding. This is also true of the honey harvested.

As you become familiar with your colony's diet, you will be able to identify the major ingredient in their honey by color alone. Early season honey will be a different shade to a second batch harvested later in the growing season.

During your inspection, try and locate the queen. She is about three times the size of the other bees in the colony and is normally conveniently marked with a dot for ease of identification.

When replacing each frame, be exceedingly careful not to crush adjacent bees. Before you close the box, check that the frames are straight and evenly placed.

Chapter 11 - Inspecting Your Hives

Adding the Upper Deep"

Approximately one month after installing your bees, the hive should have expanded sufficiently to allow installation of the upper brood box or upper deep. This box is identical in all aspects to the lower box.

Smoke the hive before you begin to work and inspect the frames in the existing box.

The lower box is the hive's "nursery" where your bees keep their brood. The upper box is the "pantry" where they store their food supplies. No honey is harvested from here as this acts as the storehouse from which the bees draw to survive the winter.

Removing the Entrance Reducer

The tiny entrance of the hive will be an extremely busy place in the first warm and sunny days of spring. Despite this, the entrance reducer is still very necessary.

Before nectar is in good supply, your bees will mostly be collecting pollen. And at this time, your bees (and bees from other colonies) will be hungering for a source of carbohydrates. If you remove the entrance reducer too soon, you are leaving your hive open as a target. Indeed, a stronger colony will regard the wider hive opening as an opportunity to steal any honey that may be left in a weaker hive.

Chapter 11 - Inspecting Your Hives

If you happen to see a crowd of bees at the entrance to a weaker hive, this is likely to be what is happening.

It is therefore critical to only remove the entrance reducer when nectar flow is plentiful. After nectar becomes readily available, weaker colonies will rapidly expand and quickly be able to defend their own colony.

As the days begin to get warmer, expect to see clusters of worker bees around the entrance fanning their wings to keep the hive cool.

The Queen Excluder and Honey Supers

After approximately two months, both the lower boxes should be full. This thrilling time means you are ready to "super" the hive. You are also ready to install a queen excluder.

Chapter 11 - Inspecting Your Hives

The honey supers are identical to the bottom boxes, but have a shallower depth. When full, a super may weigh 30-40 lbs. / 13.6-18.14 kg.

The queen excluder is a screen that sits directly on top of the upper deep. The slats in the screen allow the worker bees to pass through, but the queen is too large to fit.

Simply lay the excluder over the deep. Put the first super on top of the excluder, and then the inner and outer covers on as usual.

When the bees fill the first super, open the hive and inspect the lower boxes (or deeps). These should be quite heavy by now. Next, add the second super.

When this is full, you will be ready for your first honey harvest.

Ventilation and Cooling

Bees are amazing in their ability to manage conditions in the hive. During hot and humid weather, don't be surprised to find the exterior of your hives covered in a "bee curtain."

This living blanket of worker bees is made up of individual bees vigorously fanning their wings to cool the hive. The joint effort is so impressive, you can feel the breeze they create.

Chapter 11 - Inspecting Your Hives

At the height of the hot season, however, it's a good idea to give your bees some help by installing a ventilation rim at the top of the hive.

This is a simple frame outfitted with screened holes that sits on top of the upper super and under the inner and outer covers. It is a simple but effective method which improves ventilation.

Dealing with Bee Stings

When a bee delivers a sting, both the barbed stinger and the venom sack tear away from the bee's body and become embedded in the insect's target. Venom continues to pump even after the bee has fallen off.

When you are stung, use your fingernail to scrape the barb out of your skin. Don't try to pinch it out. You will squeeze the venom sack and cause even more of the poison to be injected into your system.

Keep an EpiPen handy even if you are not allergic to bee stings. This auto-injection device delivers epinephrine and counteracts dangerous and even life-threatening allergic reactions to bee stings.

An EpiPen can only be purchased with a prescription. However, if you explain to your doctor that you are a beekeeper, you should have no difficulty obtaining the paperwork you need.

Chapter 12 – Harvesting Your Honey

For new beekeepers, a small first-year harvest is the norm. During the first month, the bees are busying building honeycomb. Accordingly, actual honey production is delayed.

Providing your hives survive the winter, you can expect to at least double the amount of honey harvested from year one in year two.

A Word of Sticky Warning

Before beginning the extraction process, be prepared for everything in your workplace to be sticky. Honey manages to drip everywhere no matter how careful you may be.

Most everything you touch while you are working will become coated. If honey drips on the floor, you'll track the sticky stuff all over the area in nothing flat. Only advice is to keep a bucket of water nearby - and rinse your hands frequently!

Get everything ready before you start work. Therefore, once you become sticky, you handle as little equipment as possible.

Try to keep pets and small children out of the area.

Additionally, be prepared for a thorough clean-up afterwards - or you will be inviting other, less welcome insect activity, into your life.

Chapter 12 – Harvesting Your Honey

The Debate Over Honeycomb

Honeycomb is itself a feat of insect engineering. The perfectly constructed hexagonal cells are used by the bees to raise their larvae and to store honey and pollen. Building honeycomb is, however, incredibly labor intensive for the bees.

To create 1 lb. / 500 grams of wax, the bees must consume 8.4 lbs. / 4 kg of honey. The standard procedure over the last 150 years has been to harvest the honey in a way that the beeswax is preserved and then returned to the hive. Indeed, this has been the standard procedure for more than 150 years.

Chapter 12 – Harvesting Your Honey

Traditionally, the empty or drawn combs are stored over the winter and returned to the bees to be refilled when the weather warms.

However, there is a significant risk that wax moths and small hive beetles will infest the honeycomb during winter storage.

Whilst many beekeepers choose to combat these pets with chemicals, there is a real push to break with this practice. This is in response to concerns regarding colony collapse disorder.

Chapter 12 – Harvesting Your Honey

Anything that can be done to protect bees from exposure to toxins is considered positive.

For this reason, it is becoming increasingly common to re-use the comb after the mid-season honey harvest - but to destroy the material rather than recycle it at the end of the summer.

While this practice might somewhat reduce the first honey harvest of the following year, overall it is more protective of the general health of the colony.

Removing the Frames from the Hive

When you are ready to remove frames full of honey from your supers, approach the hive as if you were doing a regular inspection.

Wearing your protective clothing, use the smoker to calm the bees and to drive them lower into the hive ready for when the inner cover is removed. With your hive tool, pry the frames loose and gently remove the bees.

Take the frames inside, and allow them to sit for a week.

This will give any excess moisture time to evaporate. Bees store honey in capped wax cells in the honeycomb. To harvest the honey, the caps or tops of the cells must be removed.

Chapter 12 – Harvesting Your Honey

Uncapping the Frames

Honeycomb is an invaluable resource to a beekeeper whether you opt to re-use it for a single season or to attempt to store the comb over the winter.

Certainly, within a single year, it is greatly to your advantage to return the comb to the bees to be refilled. You don't have to worry about doing any clean up once the honey is extracted. Just give the frames back to your bees and they'll take it from there.

Uncapping is typically done over an uncapping tank that collects the cast-off wax. It also allows any honey remaining in the caps to drain through to a lower chamber - here it can be collected through a honey "gate."
Always make sure to uncap both sides of the frame. The caps themselves can be collected and used to make candles

Chapter 12 – Harvesting Your Honey

or other beeswax-based products.

Tanks are designed to hold the finished frames until they are all ready to go into a device called an extractor. Commercial uncapping tanks retail for $60-$75 / £38-£48, although you can find many sites online that offer "do-it-yourself" solutions.

It is possible to simply use a serrated knife with a long blade to saw off the wax caps; but a heated uncapping knife designed specifically for working with honeycomb is more efficient. Depending on model and source, this tool will sell for $50-$125 / £32-£80.

A second tool called an uncapping fork may be necessary to remove some of the more stubborn wax caps. Forks are much less expensive, selling in a range of $10-$25 / £6-£16.

The Honey Extractor

When the combs are uncapped, they are placed in an extractor to be spun in one of two ways; tangentially or radially.

In a tangential extractor, the honey is only spun out in one direction. Therefore, the frames must be removed, flipped, and spun again. While the price for these units is lower, they represent twice the work, especially if you are considering using a hand-cranked model.

Chapter 12 – Harvesting Your Honey

Radial extractors fling the honey out of both sides of the frame at once and are probably the most popular choice. Both hand-cranked and motorized versions are readily available.

The mechanical version outfitted with speed control is an excellent option since the operator can begin slowly while the combs are heavy with honey and then speed up the rotation as they empty. This also helps to minimize any damage to the combs.

Extractors vary in price by capacity. Some won't accept deep frames, while others offer upgrade options to expand capacity.

A "beginner's" hand-cranked two-frame extractor retails for approximately $300 / £195, while the nine-frame equivalent is roughly $500 / £325. A powered nine-frame

Chapter 12 – Harvesting Your Honey

unit jumps to $750 / £488.

Not all models come with legs. This can add as much as $50 / £32 to the price of any extractor you are considering.

Power conversion kits for hand-cranked units retail for $250-$350 / £163-£228.

With any extractor unit, the honey drips to the bottom of the tank where it is strained into a drain or honey gate. Typically, honey is strained through three progressively finer filters of 600, 400, and 200 microns each.

The honey flows into a bottling bucket. This is also outfitted with a drain or honey gate at the bottom, allowing the honey to be drawn off into sterile jars.

Honey can be pasteurized by heating the liquid for 30 minutes at a temperature of 140 degrees F / 60 degrees C before pouring. However, this is not generally recommended as pasteurization tends to damage the flavor.

Grading and Storing Honey

Honey is graded by color ranging from light, to amber, and dark.

These hues do not necessarily reflect the taste of the honey.

Chapter 12 – Harvesting Your Honey

Generally, darker honey has a higher mineral content (potassium, chlorine, sulfur, manganese, iron, magnesium, and sodium). Some nutritionists claim this offers higher health benefits.

Honey made from flower nectar is called "blossom honey". Clover and fruit tree blossom honey are considered the sweetest and mildest. Wild forest honey has a stronger taste and is considered more nutritious and "medicinal" – it may be used to treat allergies, lower inflammation, heal wounds, and promote better digestive health.

Store your honey at room temperature away from sunlight.

Chapter 13 – The Changing Seasons

Although opinions vary on the best way to prepare your hives for the winter months, there's general agreement that the colder seasons of the year are an anxious time for beekeepers.

Without pollen to gather, and relying only on stored honey and supplemental feeding from you, your bees face the challenge of surviving until the spring thaw.

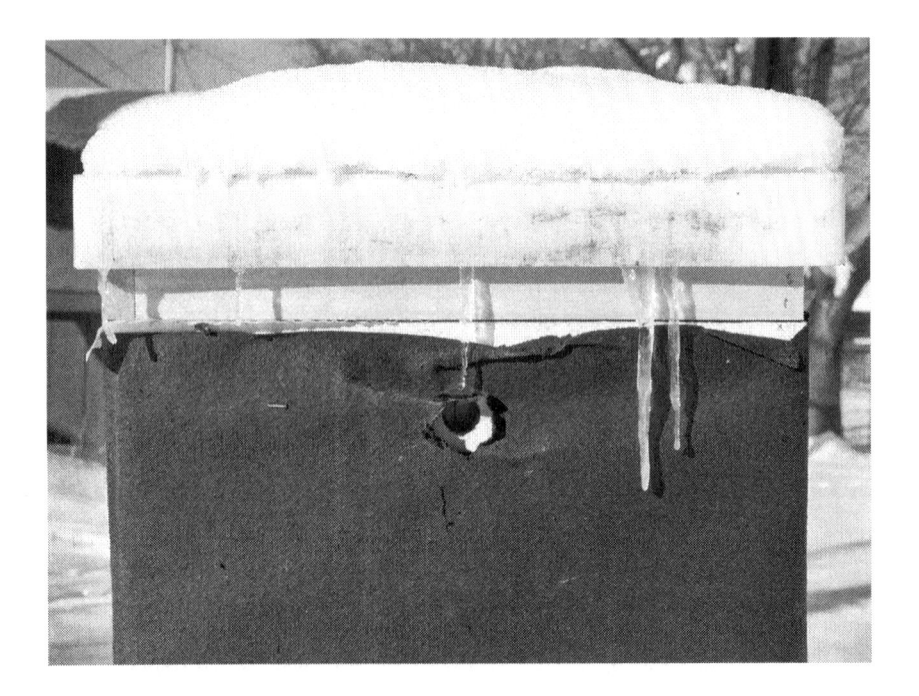

Survival of the Colony

No matter what you do, it's impossible to ensure that all your bees will survive the winter. The natural flow is that

Chapter 13 – The Changing Seasons

many of the bees will die so that there are much reduced numbers throughout the cold winter seasons.

The goal is to simply keep the colony alive during the winter. The bees are then in position to rapidly build up their population numbers for a new honey-producing summer season.

Early Spring

The most dangerous time for a colony is around early March. If the bees have exhausted their stored food supply, you will need to offer them supplemental food to survive until pollen is once again plentiful.

This is also the time of year when destruction from varroa mites is most likely to occur.

Essential Winter Ventilation

Regardless of the precautions you take, a hive with a weak queen will likely not survive the winter. It is unfortunately common for beginner beekeepers to be overzealous about sealing the hive.

If you wrap your boxes too tightly, the poor ventilation will create a serious problem. To stay warm, the bees cluster together and vibrate their bodies.

Chapter 13 – The Changing Seasons

This strategy generates sufficient heat to raise the interior temperature of the hive to a cozy 95 F / 35 C.

When the rising heat hits the inner cover, however, it will form condensation if the hive is not properly ventilated. The condensation will cool and drip back down onto the bees – this will result in death.

Preparing for Winter

Take the following steps to prepare your hives for the winter:

- Put an entrance reducer in place to serve as a mouse guard. Mice love to spend the winter in a nice warm hive. While they may not hurt your bees, they will gnaw on your frames and boxes. This will inflict considerable damage. The entrance reducer is also useful to keep cold winds out of the hive.

- Remove the honey supers. They are only there to collect honey for you and do not serve the colony over the winter months.

- Remove the queen excluder. They are only useful when the honey supers are in place.

- Prepare winter sugar syrup (refer to following chapter for recipe). Lift the lower deeps and judge the amount of stored honey. Most beekeepers like to have about 70 lbs. / 31.75 kg of honey in the lower deep to carry the bees through the winter. Less than

Chapter 13 – The Changing Seasons

that, and you will need to feed your bees. Typically, it's a good idea to do at least one initial winter feed anyway. This also enables you to treat your bees against potential illnesses like mites and Nosema.

- Wrap the hive with some type of insulation. Cut holes for all the openings so none are obstructed. Roofing paper is a good choice because it absorbs the heat from the sun. Do not cut off all ventilation to the hive. Otherwise condensation will form on the interior - subjecting your bees to cold, dripping water and putting your bees at severe risk.

- If necessary, build a windbreak to protect your bees against cold fronts and winter winds.

A 96-gram bottle of Fumagillin-B costs approximately $45-$50 / £29-£33. This is sufficient to mix 21 gallons / 79.49 liters of winter sugar syrup or 10 hives.

Also use a feeding supplement like Honey B Healthy to ensure your bees are getting the required essential minerals. This product is especially effective because it stimulates the bees to feed. Again, follow the instructions on the packaging.

Sixteen fluid ounces / 480 milliliters of Honey B Healthy costs $25-$30 / £16.27-£19.52, which is sufficient to mix 24 gallons / 90.84 liters of feeding solution.

Dispense the winter syrup in hive top feeders, which take

Chapter 13 – The Changing Seasons

the place of the inner hive cover.

Checking Your Bees in Winter

Monitor the hive entrance to ensure it doesn't become blocked. Check the supplemental food supply to make sure your bees don't starve.

As spring approaches, inspect your hive on a mild day to see if there's still sealed honey in the hive and to get an idea of how many of your bees have survived.

Do not remove any frames, just observe the overall health of the hive by taking off the inner cover.

If you opt to begin feeding in the spring, don't stop until the bees have access to nectar again

Chapter 14 – Recipes for your Bees

Chapter 14 – Recipes for your Bees

It is sometimes necessary to supplement the feed of your colony of bees. There are a variety of reasons that a hive requires supplemental feeds and there are specific recipes to meet each of those needs. It is crucial that you give the appropriate recipe at the correct time.

The following recipes are designed to be used in hives where you are not going to harvest the honey for human consumption.

Do not feed sugar syrup to bees when they have a honey super in place. Sugar syrup is essentially only a short-term solution. It can be utilized to boost colony strength in early spring, or to supplement winter stores in the fall.

If bees are provided with sugar syrup when a honey super is in place, they will store it in the comb just like honey. The bees will not be able to recognize that they are different.

Be aware that a colony that is strong enough to have a honey super in place is not in need of any supplemental feeding – no syrup, no medicines. A strong colony collects everything that is needs plus more.

Recipes are designed for colonies that are weaker and in need of your support. It is exactly these colonies that are not able to have a honey super in place.

Chapter 14 – Recipes for your Bees

The Problem with Honey

Surprisingly, honey is not the best food to give as a supplement to bees. Essentially, honey is bee food that has been processed for its preservation. Honey contains substances that bees are unable to digest.

It is important to only re-feed honey to the same hive it was harvested from. So, be certain that you know where the honey has come from. Never give honey that has been bought from a store since this may contain AFB (American Foul Brood) or other similar spores. These are perfectly safe for humans to consume but can be fatal for bees.

Bees Love Sugar Syrup

Bees prefer to eat nectar. This makes an artificial nectar the preferred choice by bees! You can make a sugar syrup to supplement the honey they have stored – this can prevent starvation. Sugar syrup can also help to encourage the drawing of the comb or to support rearing of the brood.

Importantly, note that while sugar syrup is the better source of bee feed, bees should always be left with plenty of honey in storage. The sugar syrup is simply a good supplement.

Note that all sugar syrup should be made with white cane sugar. Raw sugar, brown sugar and molasses can be

Chapter 14 – Recipes for your Bees

damaging to bees or be difficult for them to digest. If using powdered sugar, check the list of ingredients as some contain anti-caking agents that can be dangerous to bees.

Note that weights do not have to be too accurate as the bees will not be affected by the specifics of sugar concentration.

Supplement Spring Feeding

One to one syrup (or 1:1) can be used for supplemental spring feeding and can help to encourage drawing of the comb.

- 1-part sugar (by weight)
- 1-part water (by weight)

Simply dissolve one pound of sugar into one pint of water. Stir the sugar into room temperature water. Continue stirring until the sugar has dissolved.

Although you can reduce the time to dissolve by using hot water, be certain that you do not allow the sugar solution to boil.

Some beekeepers recommend boiling the water first in a pan with a lid. This is to kill any fungus and bacteria. Then remove from the heat before stirring in the sugar. Also, use a sterilized spoon (immerse in boiling water). Ensure that the sugar solution is room temperature before giving to the bees.

Chapter 14 – Recipes for your Bees

Note that the sterile sugar solution will remain clean and clear for up to two weeks using this method.

When prepared, one volume of water plus one volume of sugar will provide approximately 1.5 volumes of syrup.

One two-liter bottle of water plus one cup of water mixed with 5 pounds of sugar will produce just less than two 2-liter bottles of 1:1 sugar syrup.

Supplement Winter Feeding

The following recipe is 2:1 syrup and is optimal for the winter. You may give it during fall (after the last honey harvest), or when the bees do not have sufficient store of honey.

- 2-parts sugar (by weight)
- 1-part water (by weight)

The two parts of sugar will not dissolve in room temperature water. You will need to mix the sugar into near-boiling water. But it is essential that you do not allow the water to boil – otherwise the sugar will caramelize.

Bring a pan of water to the boil, then remove from the heat. Next, stir in the sugar with a spoon that has been sterilized with boiling water.

Check that the solution is room temperature before

Chapter 14 – Recipes for your Bees

supplying to the bees.

In the past, beekeepers have added cream of tartar to the syrup to prevent re-crystallization of the sugars. It has since been found that the cream of tartar harms the bees, so it is obviously to be avoided.

Some beekeepers add a very small amount of vitamin C as the acid (ascorbic acid) changes the pH to 4.5. This impedes crystallization and acts as an antioxidant and general boost for the bees.

You will need approximately 2 gallons / 7.57 liters of the mixed syrup per hive to get your bees through the winter.

2:1 syrup produces a final volume of syrup that is approximately double that of the liquid. For example, 2 kg of sugar in 1 liter of water will generate 2 liters of syrup.

For the first winter feeding, medicate the syrup with Fumagillin-B to protect against Nosema, a stress-related illness which causes your bees to develop dysentery.

Follow the instructions on the Fumagillin-B packaging to add the medication to the winter syrup.

Chapter 14 – Recipes for your Bees

Stimulate Brood Rearing

It is possible to stimulate brood rearing by simulating a nectar flow. This can be accomplished with a One to Two Syrup (1:2 syrup).

- 1-part sugar (by weight)
- 2 parts water (by weight)

Just mix the sugar into room temperature water.

Dry Pollen Substitute

Occasionally, it may be that there is a shortage of pollen. Or you may try and use a pollen substitute to promote the raising of the brood.

Despite the name, pollen substitutes are not really substitutes for authentic fresh pollen, but they can help as supplements.

Dry pollen substitutes are placed directly into the hive – or put in bird feeders to attract local bees.

- 3-parts soy flour (by weight) – use expeller-processed soybean flour
- 1-part brewer's yeast (by weight)
- 1-part nonfat dry milk (by weight) – do not use instant milk.

Chapter 14 – Recipes for your Bees

Combine the powders together. Sometimes the bees are reluctant to consume the pollen substitute. It can be made more appealing to the bees by adding a small amount of vitamin C. Add 1 teaspoon per 5 cups of powder. If you are unable to source a powdered vitamin C, crush a vitamin C tablet into powder and then mix in.

Pollen Patty

It is easy to make a pollen patty. Simply combine the dry pollen substitute with enough 2:1 syrup to make a dough like consistency.

Grease Patties

Grease patties containing essential oils work as an effective defense against varroa mites and tracheal mites. However, a hive that is heavily infested with Varroa will not be helped by grease patties as the bees will be too weak to consume them.

A grease patty helps to control the mite in two distinct ways. The first is that the grease tends to cover the bees meaning that they are coated in a slippery surface. The mites find it difficult to attach themselves to the bees. The second defense is the essential oils which have a repellent effect on the mites.

Chapter 14 – Recipes for your Bees

It is beneficial to provide grease patties all year round – even those without essential oils help although to a lesser extent.

Note that patties made with essential oils should never be used when honey supers are in the hive. Indeed, when you have a honey super in place, use a simple grease patty with no essential oils.

The inclusion of mineral salt provides the bees with essential minerals that they would ordinarily collect from the environment. Consequently, the addition of mineral salt it especially important during the winter. The sugar makes the patties more appealing to the bees.

Make the patties in advance and freeze. Beekeepers normally place about 4 or 5 small patties (approximately 2 ounces each) on the top bars and an additional one just inside the entrance to the hive.

Simple Grease Patty;

- 1-part solid vegetable shortening (by volume)
- 2-parts white sugar (by volume)

Combine sugar and shortening until well mixed in. Divide into approximately quarter cup portions and store any extras in the freezer (divide between sheets of wax paper).

Grease Patty with Mineral Salt

Chapter 14 – Recipes for your Bees

- 2 lbs. solid vegetable shortening
- 3 lbs. white sugar
- 1 lb. 1:2 syrup
- 1/3 cup pulverized mineral salt

Mix together until well combined.

Grease Patty with Essential Oils and Mineral Salt

- 2 lbs. solid vegetable shortening
- 3 lbs. white sugar
- 1 lb. 1:2 syrup
- 1/3 pulverized mineral salt
- 3 tablespoons of wintergreen oil

Simply combine all ingredients together. Note that it is compulsory to wear protective gloves when touching wintergreen oil. This is because wintergreen oil can be poisonous to humans when absorbed through the skin.

Chapter 15 – Honey Bee Health

Chapter 15 – Honey Bee Health

There are numerous good quality books specific to issues of Honey Bee health - including material on parasites and predators.
The following is intended as a basic overview of the more common ailments with which a backyard beekeeper must deal.

For more exhaustive material on this subject, consult *Raising Healthy Honey Bees* by Randy Carl Lynn and Todd Cooney or *Honey Bee Pest and Diseases* by Farzana Perveen.

Chapter 15 – Honey Bee Health

Varroa Mites

There are two forms of the parasitic varroa mites, Varroa destructor and Varroa jacobsoni.

The pests were first discovered in 1904 and are now present on all the continents except Australia. Varroa mites were found in the United States in 1987 and in Great Britain in 1992.

They attach themselves to the bee's thorax and are visible as small reddish-brown spots. The mites feed on bees in any stage of their metamorphosis and infect them with a virus that causes wing deformation.

Varroa mites have had a devastating effect on feral bee colonies and can be problematic for apiaries. They are a threat particularly during periods when hive strength is reduced - specifically the cold winter months.

Various chemicals are used to control varroa mites including amitraz, fluvalinate, coumaphos, thymol, sucrose octanoate esters, oxalic acid, and formic acid.

More natural approaches include dusting with powdered sugar. This encourages cleaning behavior that dislodges the mites. Also, the use of screened bottom boards can help to make sure that dislodged mites can fall away.

Since varroa mites are especially attracted to drone brood, many beekeepers will sacrifice the brood to inhibit infestation.

Chapter 15 – Honey Bee Health

Tracheal Acarine Mites

The small parasitic mite, Acarapis woodi, infests the Honey Bee's airways. Mature females travel from one bee to the next by climbing out onto the hairs and then dropping onto a younger host. Once on a host, the mites crawl into the air passages and begin laying eggs.

The first known infestation occurred early in the 20th century in Britain and the pests entered the United States from Mexico in 1984.

The most common method of control is to give the bees grease patties (see previous chapter). The patties are placed on the top bars of the hive where the bees feed on the material, picking up bits of the slick shortening on their bodies. This prevents the mite's ability to identify new hosts.

Disrupting their life cycle in this fashion and using menthol, either in vapor form or as an ingredient in the grease patties, can bring acarine mites under control.

There is also an option of using the hybrid Buckfast bee, which is acarine mite resistant.

Nosema

The microsporidian, *Nosema apis*, attacks the bees' intestine. During the winter, when the bees cannot leave the hive to take cleansing flights for elimination, this leads to the development of dysentery.

Chapter 15 – Honey Bee Health

The standard treatments are increased ventilation in the hive and the use of the antibiotic fumagillin.

Small Hive Beetle

The dark-colored *Aethina tumida* is a dark beetle indigenous to Africa. It was first found in beehives in the Western Hemisphere in Florida in 1998. The insects spread rapidly, crossing the country to California by 2006.

Since the beetles' pupation takes place outside the hive and in the ground, control measures that keep ants out of the hive are also effective against these pests. Some beekeepers use diatomaceous earth around the hives to further disrupt the beetles' lifecycle.

The chemical fipronil, commonly used against roaches, can be deployed against the beetles if placed inside corrugated cardboard. The beetles can crawl into the space, but bees cannot.

Wax Moths

While the wax moth, *Galleria mellonella*, will not harm the bees themselves, these insects do destroy honeycomb and in the process, contaminate honey and kill bee larvae.

Wax moths are especially problematic in comb stored over the winter in warmer climates. However, these moths cannot survive cold storage or freezing. The optimal temperature for the wax moth is 90 F / 30 C.

Chapter 15 – Honey Bee Health

Typically, healthy and strong hives are not endangered by wax moths. The bees themselves clean out the comb and in the process, destroy any moth larvae or webs present.

Foulbrood

The most destructive and widespread bee brood disease, American foulbrood or AFB is caused by the rod-shaped *Paenibacillus larvae* bacterium. Bee larvae ingest the bacterium's spores, which germinate in the gut of the larvae allowing the bacteria to begin to grow.

Larvae older than three days are safe, but infected larvae die inside their sealed cells. The AFB spores are so hardy they can remain viable for as long as 40 years. AFB is highly infectious.

The European variant is caused by the bacterium *Melissococcus plutonius* and is less serious than AFB. The European spores do not survive as long, and an infestation is regarded as a "stress" disease."

There is no real reliable treatment for AFB due to the resistance of the spores to desiccation. Many state apiary inspectors in the United States require that diseased hives be burned.

A less radical approach involves burning the frames and comb while only scorching the hive interior, bottom board and covers.

Chapter 15 – Honey Bee Health

Some beekeepers dip the parts of the hive in hot paraffin wax or bleach to combat the spores. Sterilization with ethylene oxide gas in a closed chamber is also possible.

Chalkbrood

The fungal disease chalkbrood is caused by *Ascosphaera apis*. This is a fungus that consumes all available food and causes the death of bee larva before then consuming the larva itself.

Chalkbrood is seen most often during wet spring seasons and can generally be prevented or cured by increasing hive ventilation.

Stonebrood

Three types of fungus are responsible for stonebrood: *Aspergillus fumigatus*, *Aspergillus flavus*, and *Aspergillus niger*.

The fungus causes brood to become mummified. The spores hatch in the gut and grow rapidly, killing the larva, which blackens and becomes very tough.

Worker bees clean out the infected brood and recovery is possible if the colony is strong.

Chapter 15 – Honey Bee Health

Other Health Threats

Bees may be susceptible to any number of viral diseases, which are extremely difficult to treat. They are also at risk from exposure to pesticides used agriculturally. Due to the distance at which bee's forage, they often fly into areas where spraying takes place.

This is, unfortunately, out of the beekeepers' control. However, jurisdictions exist, ensuring that beekeepers have the right to be informed of such activities.

My recommendation would be that if you live near working farms, you develop a friendly relationship with the owners and ask to be told when spraying will occur. This means that you can keep your bees inside the hive until the pesticide dissipates.

The Risk of Colony Collapse Disorder

Colony collapse disorder was first identified in Florida in 2006. It is a poorly understood threat to Honey Bee populations that causes the worker bees in hives to suddenly disappear.

Since that time, the phenomenon has been seen in spots throughout Europe, with some reports of cases in Asia. There are multiple theories to explain CCD.

Likely culprits include environmental stress, an unknown pathogen, mites, or indiscriminate use of pesticides. Less credible theories suggest genetically modified crops or even

Chapter 15 – Honey Bee Health

largescale use of cell phones as the underlying cause.

The most recent theories, however, point to a dual infection of invertebrate iridescent virus type 6 and *Nosema ceranae*.

Afterword
Afterword

Now that you've had a basic introduction to honey bee husbandry, the decision is up to you. Was this simply a pleasant exercise in learning more about a topic you've always found interesting or is this the beginning of further study and practical action?

Your 'next step' may be to contact a beekeeper or beekeeping club. Maybe you could even arrange to spend some time in a bee yard. This will be a fantastic peak into this fascinating endeavor.

Consider the "shock and awe" factor of working with a hive for the first time. Whilst the industrious hum of bees is very soothing to an established beekeeper, the realization of just how many thousands of bees living in those hives can be terrifying at first.

Afterword

Are bees capable of getting angry en masse? Of course - they are. And you are capable of learning how to ensure that doesn't happen!

Keeping bees isn't a one-sided operation. The honey bees will respond to the way they are treated; just like every other living creature on the planet.

Clearly if you are severely allergic to bee stings, this is not the hobby for you. But there is no need to fear Honey Bees. They're out to get the nectar, not to sting hapless humans.

The relationship between man and Honey Bee is long. In its modern iteration, beekeeping is quite benevolent. This is thanks to L.L. Langstroth. We now know how to cultivate honey in such a way that the honeycomb is preserved. This allows for larger and more productive colonies.

Especially, if you learn to use all the products of your hives, including the beeswax, beekeeping is a richly rewarding pastime. It is a natural companion to any type of organic gardening, and a terrific way to contribute to the health of the environment.

Clearly, there aren't enough good things I can say about including beekeeping in your life. I find it oddly meditative. When I am working with my bees, including just spending time with them, I find that hours pass like minutes. It isn't so much that the hives require that much working time, it's that I have come to crave that much time with my bees!

If you decide to embark on this richly rewarding behavior,

Afterword

good luck to you and to your hives. I hope you will cultivate not just excellent honey producers, but also new friends.

While beekeeping can be learned and practiced as a solitary endeavor, it also lends itself well to group efforts where sites, equipment, and even bees can be shared.

Regardless, approach beekeeping for what it is – truly rewarding - and an invaluable way to help honey bees, an extraordinarily humble creature that our whole world relies upon.

Relevant Websites

Relevant Websites

Amazing Feats of Urban Beekeeping
www.popularmechanics.com/home/how-to/g60/urban-beekeeping-47093003/

The American Apitherapy Society, Inc.
www.apitherapy.org

Backyard Beekeeping
www.outdoorplace.org/beekeeping/citybees.htm

Basic Beekeeping Equipment
www.uky.edu/Ag/Entomology/ythfacts/4h/beekeep/basbeeeq.htm

Bee Culture: The Magazine of American Beekeeping
www.beeculture.com

Beekeeping 101: DIY Beekeeping, Supplies, Plans, and Ideas
www.popularmechanics.com/home/lawn-garden/how-to/g56/diy-backyard-beekeeping-47031701/

Beekeeping Supplies - Brushy Mountain Bee Farm
www.brushymountainbeefarm.com

Beesource
www.beesource.com

Beginning Beekeeping
www.beginningbeekeeping.com

British Beekeepers Association (BBKA)

Practical Guide to Beekeeping - Beekeeping Made Easy

Relevant Websites

www.bbka.org.uk

European Professional Beekeepers Association
www.professional-beekeepers.eu

Honey Extractors - Which One to Get?
thebeejournal.blogspot.com/2010/06/honey-extractors-which-one-to-get.html

How Do Bees Make Honey?
insects.about.com/od/antsbeeswasps/f/beesmakehoney.htm

How to Eat Comb Honey
www.honeybeesuite.com/how-to-eat-comb-honey/

How to Harvest Honey
www.urbanfarmonline.com/urban-livestock/bee-keeping/harvest-honey.aspx

How to Render Beeswax from Honeycomb
montanahomesteader.com/render-beeswax-honeycomb/

How You Can Help the Bees
www.huffingtonpost.com/omega-institute-for-holistic-studies/how-you-can-help-the-bees_b_6925960.html

London Beekeepers Association
www.lbka.org.uk

National Bee Supplies
www.beekeeping.co.uk

Natural Beekeeping Trust

Relevant Websites

www.naturalbeekeepingtrust.org

NSW Apiarists' Association
www.nswaa.com.au

Queensland Beekeepers Association
qbabees.org.au

Scottish Beekeepers Association
www.scottishbeekeepers.org.uk

Ulster Beekeepers Association
www.ubka.org

Welsh Beekeepers Association
www.wbka.com

Glossary

Glossary

Please note this is far from an exhaustive glossary of bee-related terminology. The following words have been defined in an effort to augment the existing text and to provide a novice beekeeper with a working vocabulary.

A

Abdomen - A bee's abdomen is the third region of the body which contains the honey stomach, intestine, and reproductive organs among others. This is also the location of both the wax glands and the stinger.

Abscond - Bees are said to abscond when they leave the hive in response to an extreme degree of stress ranging from disease to even a physical threat like fire.

Alarm pheromone - Released by worker bees as a means of communication during an emergency.

American foulbrood (AFB) - A brood disease caused by the bacterium *Paenibacillus*.

Apiary - The location where colonies of honey bees are kept. May also be referred to as the bee yard.

Apiculture - The art, science, and pastime of keeping and husbanding honey bees.

Apis mellifera - The scientific name for the species of honey bee most common in the United States.

Glossary

B

Bee space - The space between the frames of a hive in which the bees live. Sufficiently small to allow the frames to be disengaged from the propolis and removed without damaging the honeycomb. Measures .25 inches / 0.6 cm to .38 inches / 1 cm.

Beeswax - A mixture of organic compounds secreted by bees that is used to mold the cells of the honeycomb. Beeswax has a melting point of 144-147 F / 62-64 C.

Bee veil - The cloth or wire net used to cover the face, head, and neck of the beekeeper as a protection against stings.

Bee yard - The location where colonies of honey bees are kept.

Bottom board - The floor of a beehive, typically made of screened material.

Brood - The general term for eggs, larvae, and pupae of honey bees.

Brood chamber - Also called a brood box or "deep." This is the lower part of the hive where the brood is raised.

C

Capped brood - During the non-feeding pupal phase of brood development, the cells are sealed or "capped" with wax and referred to as "capped brood."

Glossary

Cappings - The covering on filled honeycomb that is sliced away to open the cells during the process of extracting honey.

Cell - A single compartment of honeycomb. Six-sided (hexagonal) in shape.

Cleansing flight - Short flights taken out of the hive by bees to void their feces.

Cluster - Bees that are grouped and hanging together to generate warmth.

Colony - Adult bees and their developing brood that live together in a single community known as a hive.

Colony Collapse Disorder - A condition suspected to be driven by a virus that causes the adult bees in a hive to die leaving only the queen and a few young bees alive.

Comb - Six-sided beeswax cells in a sheet in which bees store pollen, honey, and brood.

Comb Foundation - A sheet of plastic or beeswax made commercially embossed with cell bases on both sides. Used in lieu of natural comb that has been stored or to replace comb inadvertently damaged during the extraction process.

Creamed Honey - Honey which has been placed in controlled conditions to allow crystallization to occur.

Crystallization - Also known as honey granulation. A

Glossary

natural phenomenon where honey turns from a liquid to a semi-solid state with granular composition. After being extracted from the honeycomb, honey tends to crystallize much faster than if it were in the wax cells.

D

Dancing - Repetitive movements used as a means of communication by bees on a comb seeking to locate food and potential home sites.

Dividing - Take a single colony and dividing or splitting it to form one or more units.

Drifting - When bees go to a colony that is not their own.

Drone - A male honey bee.

Drone Congregation Area – This is about ½ to 1 mile up in the air. It is where drones from various neighboring colonies congregate and wait for queens to mate.

E

Entrance reducer - A device made of metal or wood that serves to reduce the size of a hive's entrance to allow the bees to more easily defend their home against intruders and to protect the colony from exposure to wind and the elements. Can also serve as a deterrent against vermin, like mice, during the cold months.

Glossary

European Foulbrood (EFB) - An infectious disease that affects honey bee brood. Caused by the bacterium *Melissococcus pluton*.

Extracted Honey - Honey in liquid form removed from the cone with a machine called an extractor.

F

Feeder – There are various designs of devices used to give honey bees sugar syrup for nutrition. These include hive top, entrance, pail, and in-hive frame feeders.

Forager - Worker bees that collect nectar, pollen, and water outside the hive.

Formic acid - A chemical used to treat tracheal mites and Varroa in bee hives. Dispensed in soaked pads that allows the fumes to move through the hive.

G

Granulation – Refer to crystallization.

Guard bees - Bees stationed at the front entrance of the hive who check incoming bees to ensure they are members of the hive's population.

Gums - A section of a whole tree trunk with a natural honey bee hive in the interior. Gums are moved into bee yards and tended in the same manner as hives living in

Glossary

manmade boxes.

H

Hive - A series of boxes designed for the husbandry of honey bees.

Hive tool - A tool similar in appearance to a small crowbar that is used to open hives, separate frames, and remove both wax and propolis.

Honey - The sweet material bees produce from the nectar of flowers. Honey is composed of dissolved glucose and fructose sugars with about 18% water content. There are also trace amounts of minerals, vitamins, proteins, enzymes, and sucrose.

Honey stomach - A section of an adult honey bees' abdomen used to carry nectar, honey, or water.

Hygienic bees - Bees that possess a genetic trait that leads them to remove larvae from the hive that is dead, diseased, or infested with mites.

Hymenoptera - The scientific order to which bees belong. Also includes ants and wasps.

I

Inner cover - A cover used under the top telescoping cover of a beehive.

Glossary

Italian bees - The most widely used type of honey bees in the United States. Indigenous to Italy.

L

Langstroth hive - The modern, man-made hive with movable frames. Most widely used arrangement for the husbandry of honey bees.

Larva - The second or feeding stage in the metamorphosis of a bee. The insects appear to be white grubs with no legs. Plural is larvae.

Laying worker - A worker bee that lays drone eggs. Typically present in colonies that do not have a queen.

M

Marked queen - Queens sold with a spot of paint on the upper side of their thorax to aid in location and identification.

Mating flight – One reason the queen leaves the hive is for her maiden mating flight. About a week after she hatches and has eliminated other queen hatchlings in their cells using her stinger, the new queen embarks on a mating flight. The queen flies to a 'drone congregation area'. Most queens only make this flight once – although some have been known to go back out to mate again.

Metamorphosis - Metamorphosis is a four-stage life cycle

Glossary

through which all bees pass. The stages are: egg, larva, pupa, and adult.

N

Nectar - The sweet liquid secreted by plants to which bees and other insects are attracted.

Nosema - A disease of the digestive system in honey bees. Treated with Fumagillin.

Nurse bees - Bees that are 3-10 days old that feed and care for developing brood.

O

Ocellus - The three simple eyes on top of a bee's head that function primarily as light sensors.

P

Package of Bees - A shipment of bees typically weighing 3 lbs. The bees are sent in a screened cage with a food can. The package typically contains a queen bee, secured in her own small shipping box.

Pheromone - A chemical released by one bee to trigger certain behaviors in another. The best-known example in a beehive is "queen substance," which regulates numerous behaviors within the community.

Glossary

Pollen - The male reproductive cells of flowers used as a source of protein by honey bees.

Pollen basket - The outer, flattened surface of a worker bee's hind legs. Outfitted with curved spines that allow the bee to carry pollen or propolis back to the hive.

Proboscis - The sucking tube and tongue in a bee's mouth.

Propolis - Sap or resinous material that bees collect from wound in plants and from buds. When mixed with enzymes, propolis strengthens wax comb in the hive, seals cracks, reduces entrances, and smooths out rough spots. It is essentially a construction material.

Q

Queen - A queen is a fully developed female larger than the worker bees that is capable of reproducing and secreting pheromones.

Queen Cage - The small box used when shipping a package of bees that allows the bees to become used to the queen but keeps her safe during transport. Also used when a new queen is introduced into an existing colony.

Queen cell - An elongated cell in the honeycomb for purposes of rearing a queen. It usually is an inch / 2.5 cm long with an inner diameter of 1/3 inch / 0.8 cm. The cell hangs down vertically from the comb and will either be between two frames or at the bottom of one frame.

Glossary

Queen cell cup - A rounded structure resembling a cup that workers build at the bottom of a frame to house a future queen cell. The existing queen in the colony must lay an egg in the cup before the workers complete construction of the queen cell.

Queen excluder - A grid made of plastic or metal that allows workers to move through but restricts the queen to a specific segment of the hive.

R

Rabbet - The narrow ledge built on the inside upper portion of a brood box or honey super from which the individual frames are suspended.

Re-queen - To replace the existing queen in a hive with a new queen.

Robbing - When bees in one hive steal honey from weaker colonies.

Royal jelly - A glandular secretion produced by young bees to provide especially high nutrition for the queen and for young brood.

S

Scout bees - Bees whose purpose in the hive is to search for pollen, nectar, propolis, water, or even a new location for

Glossary

the hive if the need arises.

Small hive beetle - A destructive beetle originally indigenous to South Africa now found generally in warmer areas of the United States. Especially destructive to honey bee hives.

Smoker - A device used when working a colony of bees that produces puffs of smoke that calm the insects.

Spermatheca - An internal organ of a queen bee used to store collected sperm from drone bees.

Sting - The ovipositor of a honey bee modified to deliver a load of venom as a means to defend the hive. The queen stings rival queens to kill them.

Sucrose - The main sugar found in nectar.

Super - A smaller hive box placed on top of the brood chambers where surplus honey is stored and harvested by beekeepers.

Supersedure - The replacement of an established queen by a daughter from the same hive. May be a natural or emergency occurrence.

Surplus honey - The honey stored in the upper "super" boxes of a hive. Harvested by the beekeeper since it is not required for the survival of the colony.

Swarm - Occurs when approximately half of the worker bees in a hive, some of the drones, and the queen leave to

Glossary

establish a new colony.

Swarm cell - A developing queen cell at the bottom of a frame, often created prior to a swarm.

T

Thorax - The middle section of a bee's body where the legs, wings, and most of the insect's muscle mass is located.

Tracheal Mite - The common term for Acarapis woodi, a honey bee parasite that infests the insect's trachea.

U

Uncapping Knife - A specially shaped knife that may or may not be electrically heated. Used to remove the wax sealing the individual cells in honeycomb.

V

Varroa Mite - The common name for a parasitic mite that attacks honey bees in the adult and pupal stages of development.

Virgin Queen - A queen bee that has not mated.

Varroa sensitive hygiene (VSH) - Honey bees that can locate larva infested with varroa and remove it.

Glossary

W

Wax Moth - The common name for the larvae of the moth *Galleria mellonella,* which damages brood combs.

Worker Bees - Female bees with undeveloped reproductive organs. They do all work in the colony except the laying of fertile eggs.

Worker Comb - Sections of honeycomb that contain approximately 5 cells per one inch / 2.5 cm. This is where worker bees are reared.

Index

Index

Abdomen, **19**
Africanized Honey Bee, **55**
Alfalfa, **29**
Alfalfa leafcutter bee, **12**
Allergies, **30**
American foulbrood, 134, **144**
Amos Ives Root, 71
Antenna, **18**
Apiculture, **81**
Bee Balm, **29**
Bee space, **145**
Bee Space, **89**
Bee Yard, **87**
Beehive Kit, **84**
Beeswax, **58**, **62**, **112**
Bottom Boards, **88**
Brood, **102**, **145**
Brood chamber, **145**
Buckfast Bee, **50**
Bumble Bees, **61**
Buttercup, **29**
Cappings, **146**
Carniolan Bee, **47**
Caucasian Honey Bee, 49
Chalkbrood, **135**
Clover, **28**
Colony, **22**
Colony Collapse Disorder, **14**, **15**, 136

Comb, **146**
Comb Foundation, **146**
Communication, **36**
Dance of the Honey Bee, 37
Decline of Bees, **13**
Dragonhead, **29**
Drones, **20**, **23**
Dry Pollen Substitute, **126**
Echinacea, **29**
Eggs, **24**, **102**
English Thyme, **29**
Entrance reducer, **147**
Entrance Reducer, **91**, **103**, **104**, **118**
Enzymes, **152**
EpiPen, 106
Essential Oils, **127**
European Dark Bee, **43**
European Foulbrood, **148**
Extraction, **107**, **112**
Eyesight, **20**
Feeders, **97**, **120**
Food Crops, **13**
Forager, **148**
Formic acid, **148**
Foulbrood, **134**
Frame Lifter, **90**
François Huber, **69**
Fumagillin-B, **125**, **133**

Practical Guide to Beekeeping - Beekeeping Made Easy 157

Index

Giant Honey Bee, 54
Goldenrod, 29
Granulation, **148**
Grease Patty, **127**, **132**
Gum Hives, **66**
Hive tools, **102**
Hive Top Feeder, **97**
Hiving, **93**, **94**, **97**
Honey, 30, 42, 57, 60, 64, 89, 93, 99, 102, 110, 114, 115, 122
Honey Harvest, **105**, **107**
Honey Supers, **105**, **118**
Honeycomb, 58, 89, 108, 111
Honeywort, 29
Hydration, **29**, **76**, **98**
Insurance, **32**
Ironweed, 28
Italian Honey Bee, 45
Karl Kehrle, **50**
L.L. Langstroth, 70, 139
Larvae, **24**, **102**, **150**
Lavender, 29
Leaf Hive, **69**
Lifespan, **40**
Marked queen, **150**
Mating Flight, **20**, **150**
Metamorphosis, **151**
Mice, **88**
Mineral Salt, **128**
Movable Comb Hives, **68**
Nectar, **39**, **57**, **60**, **120**, **151**

Nosema, **125**, **132**, **151**
Nurse bees, **151**
Ocellus, **151**
Ommatidia, **20**
Oranges, 29
Oregano, 28
Organic Pest Control, 29
Package of Bees, **93**
Pesticides, **16**, **136**
Pheromones, **36**, **152**
Pollen, **39**, **57**, **152**
Pollen basket, **152**
Pollen Patty, **127**
Pollination, **11**
Proboscis, **152**
Propolis, **90**, **102**, **152**
Protective Clothing, **99**
Protein Patty, **98**
Pupa, **24**
Queen, 23, **93**, **95**, **98**, **102**
Queen Cage, **152**
Queen Cell, **153**
Queen Cell Cup, **153**
Queen Excluder, **68**, **89**, 105, 118, 153
Queen Pheromones, **36**
Rabbet, **153**
Radial Extractors, **113**
Removing Frames, **110**
Re-queen, **153**
Robbing, **153**
Round Dance, **38**
Royal Jelly, **154**

Index

Russian Bee, **52**
Sage, **28**
Salvia, **28**
Scout bees, **154**
Screen Boards, **88**
Small Hive Beetle, **133**, **154**
Smoker, **95**, **100**, **101**, **154**
Sourwoods, **29**
Spring Feeding, **123**
Stinger, **106**
Stings, **20**, **35**
Stonebrood, **135**
Sugar Syrup, **94**, **122**
Sulfur Fumes, **66**
Summer, **92**
Super, **68**, **89**, **105**, **154**
Supersedure, **155**
Swarm, **155**
Swarm cell, **155**
Swarming, **24**, **27**
Tangential Extractor, **112**
Thorax, **19**
Tools, **90**

Tracheal Acarine Mite, **132**, **155**
Tulip Poplars, **29**
Tupelos, **29**
Uncapping, **111**
Upper Brood Box, **103**
Upper Deep, **103**
Varroa Mites, **131**, **156**
Venom Sack, **106**
Ventilation, **105**, **117**, **133**
Vitamin C, **127**
Waggle Dance, **38**
Wax, **21**
Wax Moth, **133**, **156**
Western Honey Bee, 42
Winter, **83**, **88**, **92**, **116**, **117**, **118**
Winter Feeding, **124**
Wintergreen oil, **129**
Worker Bees, 23
Yarrow, **29**
Yellow Hyssop, **29**
Zoning Laws, **31**

Printed in Great Britain
by Amazon